Prescott Holmes

Lives of the Presidents

Prescott Holmes

Lives of the Presidents

ISBN/EAN: 9783337397203

Printed in Europe, USA, Canada, Australia, Japan

Cover: Foto ©ninafisch / pixelio.de

More available books at **www.hansebooks.com**

LIVES OF
THE
PRESIDENTS

BY

PRESCOTT HOLMES

With Portraits and Numerous Illustrations

PHILADELPHIA
HENRY ALTEMUS
1898

PREFACE.

WE have here endeavored to acquaint young people with the story of the lives and attainments of the men who achieved the highest civic honor in the gift of the people; and to explain, in a necessarily brief narrative, the history of our political parties, the issues involved in their several contests, and their differing administrations.

The youth of the present is the *President* of the future; and an intelligent understanding of the rights and duties of citizenship is an imperative feature of his education. He will perceive that honest differences of opinion have ever prevailed, and that most of these have been settled by judicious compromises under constitutional limitations. The slavery question submitted itself to the arbitration of the sword, and was worsted; and the sin and stain of slavery was forever removed from our country.

We have attempted to describe the things which have been accomplished in order that the young patriot may have the warning and the promise in the things yet to be done. At the cost of much blood and treasure is crystalized the Nation's motto, *E Pluribus Unum.* Let us hope and act so that it will be always " now, and forever."

THE DECLARATION OF INDEPENDENCE READ TO THE ARMY.

CONTENTS.

	PAGE.
GEORGE WASHINGTON	9
JOHN ADAMS	35
THOMAS JEFFERSON	46
JAMES MADISON	67
JAMES MONROE	79
JOHN QUINCY ADAMS	97
ANDREW JACKSON	103
MARTIN VAN BUREN	115
WILLIAM HENRY HARRISON	123
JOHN TYLER	125
JAMES K. POLK	135
ZACHARY TAYLOR	144
MILLARD FILLMORE	155
FRANKLIN PIERCE	157
JAMES BUCHANAN	165
ABRAHAM LINCOLN	192
ANDREW JOHNSON	207
ULYSSES S. GRANT	215
RUTHERFORD B HAYES	233
JAMES A. GARFIELD	241
CHESTER A. ARTHUR	246
GROVER CLEVELAND	254
BENJAMIN HARRISON	265
WILLIAM MCKINLEY	269

WASHINGTON IN 1772, AT THE AGE OF FORTY.

LIVES OF THE PRESIDENTS.

GEORGE WASHINGTON—1789–1797.

GEORGE WASHINGTON, the first President, was born in Virginia, February 22, 1732. His ancestors emigrated to Virginia in the time of Cromwell (1657). His father died when he was ten years old, leaving a comfortable property to his mother and five children. She was a wise and prudent woman, and trained her family to be industrious and economical. His education was conducted partly by his mother and partly at one of the ordinary schools of the province. It was the usual middle-class education, but it included enough of mathematics to enable Washington to act as a land-surveyor. His boyhood showed many evidences of that methodical precision which was always one of his characteristics. He wrote a neat, stiff hand; he compiled "Rules of Behavior in Company and Conversation;" he surveyed the fields and plantations about the school where he was staying, and entered his measurements and calculations in a field-book with great exactness. In athletic exercises he was always foremost, and it was a favorite diversion of his to form his schoolmates into companies, and engage them in sham fights. His ambition was to enter the navy; but his mother objected, and he began his work of land-surveying. At sixteen he was employed to examine the valleys of the Alleghany mountains—a task which was continued during the next three years, and performed with skill and completeness. It was no light or easy task, for the country was a wilderness, and the severities of the weather had no mitigation in those wild passes and unsheltered glens. It was only for a few weeks at a time that he could endure this life of hardship and deprivation; but after an interval of rest and comfort, he would again seek the desert, carrying his instruments of science into the region of savage mountains, and the neighborhood of savage men.

When Washington was about nineteen, Virginia was divided into military districts, as a measure of protection against the advance of the French. Over each division an adjutant-general, with the rank of major, was appointed. Washington was commissioned to one of these districts, and set to work to study military tactics. He was so good a soldier two years later that, when the number of military divisions in Virginia was reduced to four, he was still left in command of one, and in this capacity had to train and instruct officers, to inspect men, arms, and accoutrements, and to establish a uniform system of manœuvres. When he was twenty-one, he was doing the work of an experienced major-general; and was selected by Governor Dinwiddie for a service which demanded great skill as well as daring. He was required to make his way across a mountainous desert, inhabited by Indians whose friendship could hardly be depended on; to penetrate to the frontier stations of the French; and to bring back information concerning their position and military strength, together with an answer from the French commander as to why he had invaded the British dominions during a time of peace. The expedition was all the more onerous as winter was coming on. It was October 31, 1753, ere Washington started; it was the middle of November when, with an interpreter, four attendants, and Christopher Gist as a guide, he followed an Indian trail into the dim mysteries of the unknown forest. The path took the little company into the wilderness, and carried them over deep ravines and swollen streams, made worse by the sleet and snow which then began to fall; and at length brought them, after a hurried ride of nine days, to the fork of the Ohio, where the quick glance of Washington saw the fine capabilities for planting a great commercial city, now Cincinnati.

The party swam their horses across the Alleghany, and slept that night on the bank of the river. Next morning the chief of the Delawares led them through an open country to the valley of Logstown, where they were cordially received by the Indians, with whom they planned a series of operations against the French, in the event of the latter still refusing to quit the country. Accompanied by several of the natives, Washington and his friends again set forward, and reached the French post, where the officers avowed their resolve to take possession of the Ohio. They boasted of their forts at Le Bœuf, Erie, Niagara, Toronto, and Frontenac, and said that the English would be unable, though two to one, to prevent any enterprise of the French. From this point, the Virginian envoys made their way, across creeks so swollen by the rains as to be passable only over felled trees, towards the fort of Le Bœuf, situated at Waterford. Rain and snow fell; they were often engulfed in miry swamps, and were forced to kill bucks and bears for their sustenance. On gaining Fort Le Bœuf, they found it surrounded by the rough, log-built barracks of the soldiers. In front lay 50 birch-bark canoes, and 170 boats of pine, ready for the descent of the river; while, close by, materials were collected for building more. The commander of the fort was a man of great courage, of large experience, and of so much integrity that

WASHINGTON PLANTING THE BRITISH FLAG AT FORT DUQUESNE.

he was at once feared and beloved by the savages. He refused to discuss with young Washington the abstract question of right. He had been placed there by his chief, and would execute the orders he had received. To the letter from Didwiddie which Washington delivered, requiring the evacuation of the place, he replied by a direct refusal, and an intimation of his purpose to seize every Englishman within the Ohio Valley. Having executed his commission, Washington, with his companions, turned homeward. The return was worse than the journey out; for it was now the depth of winter, and having to cross many creeks and small rivers, they suffered severely from the rigor of the season. Once, a canoe which they now had with them was driven against the rocks; at other times they were obliged to carry it across the half-frozen stream; often they waded through water which froze upon their clothes. Snow fell heavily, and a bitter frost set in. Washington and Gist separated from the others, and struck across the open country towards the fork of the Ohio, steering their way by the compass. But the deadly cold was not the only peril they had to face. Hostile Indians lay in wait for the travelers, and one fired at Washington as he passed. The Alleghany was crossed on a raft laboriously made out of trees which they had first to fell. The passage of the river was made difficult and dangerous by floating ice, and Washington, in manœvering the raft, was thrown into the benumbing current. He and his companion got to a small island, and passed the night there; in the morning the river was entirely frozen over, and they crossed on foot. On January 16, 1754,

Washington again found himself at the Virginia capital. The journal of his expedition, which was published shortly afterwards, gave a very high idea of his sagacity, self-reliance, and powers of observation; and his minute description of the fort which he had visited—of its form, size, construction, and number of cannon—advanced his reputation as a military critic. That winter's journey had brought a new actor on the stage of the world.

Dinwiddie attempted to force the French from the ground claimed by the English. Two companies were raised, and put under Washington's command with orders "to drive away, kill, and destroy, or seize as prisoners all persons, not the subjects of Great Britain, who should attempt to take possession of the lands on the Ohio River, or any of its tributaries." This expedition failed; the forces being too few and too poor to succeed. Thus the first important operation of a British army upon American soil ended in disgrace and ruin. Yet they did some good fighting, and Washington gained great honor for his wise actions and bravery. But Dinwiddie treated him so disrespectfully that he resigned. He was soon invited to become an aide to General Braddock, who was appointed by the King to take charge of all the forces then in the field.

When they set out toward Fort Duquesne with 3000 men—British regulars and Colonial troops—Braddock expected to find the French and Indians drawn up in regular lines in an open field, and he thought that he would only need to make a bold attack and they would all run. Washington told him that Indians fought by hiding behind trees and lying in wait in unexpected places, and he cautioned the English general to send out scouts in advance of the troops. But Braddock would not listen; on the contrary he exhibited towards him the most unreasoning obstinacy and most irascible temper. He knew more about fighting than this young colonial captain could tell him—until the Indians fell upon his ranks just as Washington predicted, sending bullets thick and fast into them, while the amazed Britishers saw nothing but trees at which to return fire. Many of the officers fell; Braddock himself was wounded, and Washington had to take command, and conducted the retreat in a masterly manner. He met the foe with their own weapons; he scattered his men among the trees; he rode here and there giving orders; two horses were shot from under him, and four bullets passed through his coat, but he was not harmed. He checked the advance of the French and Indians, but not until nearly half of the English troops had been killed.

This affair showed the British Government what Washington could do, and when a new force was raised he was put in command of 2000 men; but feeling deeply repulsed by the condition of the army, he resigned after the capture of Fort Duquesne in November, 1758.

The next year he married a rich and beautiful widow, Mrs. Martha Custis; she, with her two children, he took to his family mansion at Mount Vernon. He took no part in military life now, but attended to his large estates.

Thus at 27, we find Washington a country gentleman, proprietor of a plantation upon which wheat and tobacco were raised, and fisheries and brickyards carried on. He had about 125 slaves. He was a good master; and directed in his will that on his death his slaves should have their freedom. He became a member of the House of Burgesses, but seldom took any active part. When he spoke at all, it was briefly, but Patrick Henry said that he was,

WASHINGTON'S HOUSE, MOUNT VERNON.

"for solid information and sound judgment, unquestionably the greatest man in the Assembly."

The Federal Constitution is the result of the labors of a convention called at Philadelphia in May, 1787, when it was feared by many that the Union was in danger, from inability to pay soldiers who had, in 1783, been disbanded on a declaration of peace and an acknowledgment of independence; from prostration of the public credit; and from the neglect to provide for the payment of even the interest on the public debt. A large portion of the convention clung to the confederacy of the States, and advocated a revival of the old articles of confederation with additional powers to Congress. A long discussion followed, but a constitution for the people embodying a division of legislative, judicial and executive powers prevailed, and the result is now witnessed in our Federal Constitution. The Revolutionary War lasted but seven years, while the political revolution directing it lasted thirteen years. This was completed on April 30, 1789, when Washington was inaugurated as the first President under the Federal Constitution.

The meeting of the new Government was to be on March 4, 1789; but so backward were some of the States in sending representatives that it was April 6 before a quorum of both Houses could be formed. On the votes for President and Vice-President being opened and counted, it was found that Washington had received the largest number of suffrages, and John Adams the next largest. The former, therefore, stood in the position of President; the latter in that of Vice-President. It was on this way, originally, that the two chief officers of the Union were selected. The news that he had been chosen to the Presidency was communicated to Washington on April 14. He departed for the seat of Government on the 16th. His journey to New York was one continued triumph. The roads were lined with people who came out to see him as he passed.

Continuing his journey, he arrived on the banks

of the Delaware, close to the city of Trenton. The opposite shore of the river was thronged with an enthusiastic crowd. An arch, composed of laurels and hot-house flowers, spanned the bridge and on the crown of the arch, in letters of leaves and blossoms, were the words, "December 26, 1776," while on the space beneath was the sentence, "The Defender of the Mothers will be the Protector of the Daughters." Here the matrons of the city were drawn up, and, as Washington passed under the arch, a number of young girls, dressed in white and crowned with garlands, strewed flowers before him, and chanted a song of welcome.

Washington reached New York City on April 23, but the inauguration did not take place until a week later. On the morning of April 30, religious services were held in all the churches. At noon the city troops paraded before Washington's door, and soon afterwards the Committees of Congress and heads of departments arrived in their carriages. A procession was formed, and, preceded by troops, moved forward to the Old City Hall, standing on the sight of the present Custom-house. Washington rode in a state coach, and the chief officials in their own carriages. The Foreign Ministers and a long train of citizens followed; and the windows along the whole line of the route were crowded with spectators. On nearing the Hall, Washington and his suite alighted from their carriages, and passed through two lines of troops into the Senate Chamber, where the Vice-President, the Senate, and the members of the House of Representatives were assembled. John Adams, as the Vice-President, conducted Washington to a chair of state at the upper end of the room. After a solemn pause, the Vice-President rose, and informed the President that all things were prepared for him to take the oath of office. It was arranged that the oath should be administered by Robert R. Livingston, the Chancellor of the State of New York, in a balcony of the Senate Chamber, and in full view of the people assembled below.

At the appointed hour, Washington came out on the balcony, accompanied by various public officers, and by members of the Senate and House of Representatives. The President-elect was clad in a full suit of dark brown cloth, *of American manufacture*, with a steel-hilted dress sword, white silk stockings, and silver shoe-buckles; and his hair was dressed and powdered in the fashion of the day, and worn in a bag and solitaire. Loud shouts greeted his appearance. He was evidently somewhat shaken by this testimony of public affection, and, advancing to the front of the balcony, laid his hand upon his heart, bowed several times, and then retired to an arm-chair near the table. He was now supported on the right by John Adams, and on the left by Robert R. Livingston, while in the rear were several of his old friends and military companions. The Bible was held up on its crimson cushion by the Secretary of the Senate, while the Chancellor read the terms of the oath, slowly and distinctly. These were: "I do solemnly swear that I will faithfully execute the office of President of the United States, and will, to the best of my

THE INAUGURATION OF WASHINGTON.

ability, preserve, protect, and defend the Constitution of the United States." While the words were being recited, Washington kept his hand on the open Bible, and on the conclusion of the oath he solemnly responded, "I swear—so help me God!" The secretary offered to raise the Bible to his lips; but he bowed down reverently, and kissed it. The Chancellor now stepped forward, and exclaimed, "Long live George Washington, President of the United States!" A flag was run up above the cupola of the Hall; *thirteen* guns on the battery were discharged; the bells of the city burst into joyous peals; and the voices of the people again poured forth the grandest of all forms of homage.

In all governments there *must* be parties. At the beginning, we had the Republicans (now the Democrats), who desired a government republican in form and democratic in spirit, with right of local self-government and State rights ever uppermost. The Federalists desired a government republican in form, with checks upon the impulses or passions of the people; liberty, sternly regulated by law, and that law strengthened and confirmed by central authority —the authority of the National Government to be final in appeals.

Party hostilities were not manifested in the Presidential election. All bowed to the popularity of Washington, and he was unanimously nominated. He selected his cabinet from the leading minds of both parties, and while himself a recognized Federalist, all felt that he was acting for the good of all, and in the earlier years of his administration none disputed this fact.

As the new measures of the Government advanced, however, the anti-Federalists organized an opposition to the party in power. Immediate danger had passed. The Constitution worked well. The laws of Congress were respected; its calls on the States for revenue honored, and Washington devoted much of his first and second messages to showing the growing prosperity of the country, and the respect which it was beginning to excite abroad. But where there is political power, there is opposition in a free land, and the great leaders of that day neither forfeited their reputations as patriots, or their characters as statesmen, by the assertion of honest differences of opinion. Washington, Adams, and Hamilton were the recognized leaders of the Federalists, the firm friends of the Constitution. The success of this instrument modified the views of the anti-Federalists, and Madison, of Virginia, its recognized friend when it was in preparation, joined with others who had been its friends in opposing the administration, and soon became recognized leaders of the anti-Federalists. Jefferson was then on a mission to France, and not until some years thereafter did he array himself with those opposed to centralized power in the nation. He returned in November, 1789, and was called to Washington's Cabinet.

It was a great Cabinet. Thomas Jefferson, of Virginia, the author of the *Declaration of Independence*, was deservedly made Secretary of State, which is looked upon as the chief office in the gift of the administration. Alexander Hamilton, of New York, who had taken part in the battles of White Plains, Trenton, and Princeton, and in the second year of the war was made Washington's aide-de-camp and confidential military secretary, and who remained with the army till the British surrendered at Yorktown, where he was at the head of his command, was placed at the head of the Treasury.

ALEXANDER HAMILTON.

Henry Knox, of Massachusetts, took a conspicuous part in the Battle of Trenton, where he was wounded, but was no less active in the succeeding battles of Princeton, Brandywine and Germantown. He was commended for his military skill and cool, determined bravery at Yorktown; when Congress advanced him to the rank of Major-General and he took possession of New York when the British finally evacuated it in 1783. He shared intimately and constantly in all the Councils with Washington in the field, and quite naturally was appointed Secretary of War.

Edmund Randolph, who had been Governor of Virginia, and a member of the Constitutional Convention, was appointed Attorney-General. He was advanced to the office of Secretary of State when Jefferson resigned in 1794.

The first session of Congress, held in New York, sat for nearly six months. Nearly all the laws framed pointed to the organization of the Government, and the discussions were general and protracted. The Federalists carried their measures by small majorities.

Much of the second session was devoted to the discussion of the able reports of Hamilton, and their final adoption did much to build up the credit of the nation and to promote its industries. He was the author of the *protective* system. He recommended the funding of the war debt, the assumption of the State war debts by the National Government, the providing of a system of revenue for the collection of duties on imports, and an internal excise. His advocacy of a protective tariff was plain, for he declared it be necessary for the support of the Government and *the encouragement of manufacturers* that duties be laid on goods, wares, and merchandise imported.

The third session of Congress was held at Philadelphia, though the seat of the National Government had, at the previous one, been fixed on the Potomac. To complete Hamilton's financial system, a national bank was incorporated. On this project both the members of Congress and of the Cabinet were divided, but it passed, and was promptly approved by Washington. It came to be known that Jefferson and Hamilton held opposing views on many questions of government, and these influenced the action of Congress, and passed to the people, who were thus early believed to be almost equally divided on the more essential political issues. Before the close of the session, Vermont and Kentucky were admitted to the Union. Vermont was the first State admitted in addition to the original thirteen. True, North Carolina and Rhode Island had rejected the Constitution, but they reconsidered their action and came in, the former in November, 1789, and the latter in May, 1790.

The next Congress had a majority in both branches favorable to the administration. It met at Philadelphia in October, 1791. The exciting measure of the session was the Excise Act. The people of western Pennsylvania, largely interested in distilleries, prepared for armed resistance to the excise law, but at the same session a national militia law had been passed, and Washington took advantage of this to suppress the "Whisky (or Shaw's) Rebellion" in its incipiency. It was a hasty, rash undertaking, yet was dealt with so firmly that the action of the authorities strengthened the law and the respect for order.

Congress passed an apportionment bill, which based the congressional representation on the census taken in 1790, the basis being 33,000 inhabitants for each representative. The second session sat from November, 1792, to March, 1793, and was occupied in discussing the foreign and domestic relations of the country.

The most serious objection to the Constitution, before its ratification, was the absence of a distinct bill of rights, which should recognize "the equality of all men, and their rights to life, liberty and the pursuit of happiness," and the first Congress framed a bill containing twelve articles, ten of which were afterwards ratified as amendments to the Constitution. Yet State sovereignty, then imperfectly defined, was the prevailing idea in the minds of the Anti-Federalists, and they took every opportunity to oppose any extended delegation of authority from

INDEPENDENCE HALL, AS IT WAS IN 1776.

the States to the Union. They contended that the power of the State should be supreme, and charged the Federalists with monarchical tendencies. They opposed Hamilton's national bank scheme, and Jefferson and Randolph expressed the opinion that it was unconstitutional—that a bank was not authorized by the Constitution, and that it would prevent the States from maintaining banks. But when the bill of rights had been incorporated in and attached to the Constitution as amendments, Jefferson with rare political sagacity withdrew all opposition to the instrument itself, and the Anti-Federalists gladly followed his lead, for they felt that they had labored under many partisan disadvantages. The Constitution was from the first too strong for successful resistance, and when opposition was confessedly abandoned the party name was changed, at the suggestion of Jefferson, to that of Republican. The Anti-Federalists were at first disposed to call their party the Democratic-Republicans, but finally called it simply Republican, to avoid the opposite of the extreme which they charged against the Federalists. Each party had its taunts in use, the Federalists being denounced as monarchists, the Anti-Federalists as Democrats; the one presumed to be looking forward to monarchy, the other to the rule of the mob.

By 1793 partisan lines, under the names of Federalists and Republicans, were plainly drawn. Personal ambition had much to do with it, for Washington had expressed his desire to retire to private life. While he remained at the head of affairs he was unwilling to part with Jefferson and Hamilton, and did all in his power to bring about a reconciliation, but without success. Before the close of the first Constitutional Presidency, Washington became convinced that the people desired him to accept a re-election, and he was accordingly a candidate and unanimously chosen. John Adams was re-elected Vice-President, receiving 77 votes to 50 for George Clinton, of New York. The electors could not vote for Washington and Jefferson, both being from Virginia.

Soon after the inauguration, Genet, an envoy

GEORGE CLINTON.

from the French republic, arrived and sought to excite the sympathy of the United States and involve it in a war with Great Britain. Jefferson and his Republican party warmly sympathized with France, and insisted that gratitude for revolutionary favors commanded aid to France in her struggles. The Federalists, under Washington and Hamilton, favored non-intervention, and insisted that we should maintain friendly relations with Great Britain. Washington showed his usual firmness, and issued his celebrated proclamation of neutrality. This has ever since been the accepted foreign policy of the nation.

The French agitation showed its impress as late as 1794, when a resolution to cut off intercourse with Great Britain passed the House, and was defeated in the Senate only by casting the vote of the Vice-President, John Adams. Jefferson left the Cabinet the December previous, and retired to his plantation in Virginia, where he spent his leisure in writing political essays and organizing the Republican party, of which he was the acknowledged founder. Here he escaped the errors of his party in Congress, but it was a fact that his friends not only did not endorse the non-intervention policy of Washington, but that they actively antagonized it in many ways. The congressional leader in these movements was James Madison; afterwards elected to the Presidency. The policy of Britain fed this opposition. The forts on Lake Erie were still occupied by the British soldiery in defiance of the treaty of 1783; American vessels were seized on their way to French ports, and American citizens were impressed; England claiming the right during the Napoleonic wars to man her ships with her subjects wherever she could find them. To avoid a war, Washington sent John Jay as envoy to England. He arrived in June, 1794, and by

November succeeded in making a treaty. It was ratified in June, 1795, by the Senate, though there was much opposition, and the feeling between the Federal and Republican parties ran higher than ever. The Republicans denounced while the Federals congratulated Washington. Under this treaty the British surrendered possession of all American ports, and as General Wayne during the previous summer had conquered the war-tribes and completed a treaty with them, the country was again on the road to prosperity.

Jefferson retired from the Cabinet December 10, 1793. He was followed by Hamilton on January 31, 1795. His old friend General Knox quitted the War Office some time before. Washington felt considerably weakened by these retirements and could now count on but slight assistance in repelling the attacks of the Democratic party. John Jay was in England trying to adjust the old differences.

In March, 1796, a new issue was sprung in the House by a resolution requesting from the President a copy of the instructions to John Jay, who made the treaty with Great Britain.

A storm of popular fury awaited the document. Meetings were called in every town, and few dared to say a word in favor of the detested concessions. Jay was burned in effigy; Hamilton was stoned; and the British Minister at Philadelphia was insulted. The Democrats were especially loud in their condemnation. They declared that such a treaty was an act of base ingratitude to France, and involved nothing short of treason to America herself, whose watchword should at all times be hatred to monarchy and to England. Even the President was treated with little respect, and had been compelled to rebuke those who had sent some of the more violent addresses. Hamilton and others defended the treaty, by their pens, with great power and marked effect, and signs of a reaction became visible after awhile.

In spite of all the public clamor, the House, after more calm and able debates, passed the needed legislation to carry out the treaty by a vote of 51 to 48, and the treaty with England was signed by the President August 18, 1795.

It was with feelings of relief that Washington saw the termination of his Presidency approaching. His Farewell Address to the people of the United States was dated September 17, 1796, though his retirement from office was not to take place until March 4, in the following year. In this document, Washington announced the resolution he had formed to decline being considered among the number of those out of whom a new President was to be chosen. He expressed the acknowledgments he owed the country for the honors it had conferred upon him; for the steadfast confidence with which it had supported his measures, and for the opportunities he had thence enjoyed of manifesting his inviolable attachment to the institutions of the land. The Constitution established in 1787, he observed, had a just claim on the confidence and support of the entire nation. The basis of the political system was the right of the people to make and to alter their Constitutions. But the Constitution existing for the time was obligatory upon all, until changed by an explicit or authentic act of the whole people.

Tennessee was admitted to the Union on June 1, 1796. In the Presidential battle that followed, both

WASHINGTON'S GRAVE, MOUNT VERNON.

parties were confident and plainly arrayed, and so close was the result that the leaders of both were elected—John Adams the nominee of the Federalists to the Presidency, and Thomas Jefferson, the nominee of the Republicans, to the Vice-Presidency. The law which then obtained was that the candidate who received the highest number of electoral votes, took the first place, and the next highest, the second. Thomas Pinckney, of South Carolina, was the Federal nominee for Vice-President, and Aaron Burr, of New York, of the Republicans. John Adams, received 71 electoral votes; Thomas Jefferson, 68; Thomas Pinckney, 59; Aaron Burr, 30; Samuel Adams, the "silver-tongued orator" of independence fame, 15; and scattering, 37.

Upon the inauguration of John Adams, March 4, 1797, Washington retired to his family-seat at Mount Vernon, where he remained till called again by Adams to take command of the *new* army, organized in May, 1798. He died December 14, 1799, aged 68 years and was buried at Mount Vernon.

To all Americans, the life of George Washington is the noblest, the grandest, and the most influential in all our history, and ranks beside the most illustrious characters that have ever lived.

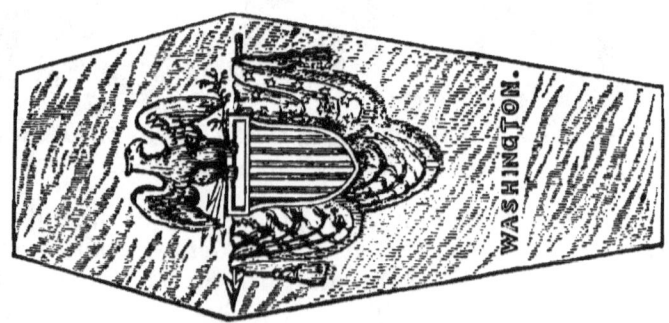

JOHN ADAMS—1797-1801.

John Adams, the second President, was born in Massachusetts on October 30, 1736. His parents were of the class, then abounding in New England, who united the profession of agriculture with some of the mechanic arts. His ancestor Henry had emigrated from England in 1632, and had established himself at Braintree with six sons, all of whom married: from one President Adams descended, and from another that Samuel Adams who, with John Hancock, was by name proscribed by an Act of the British Parliament, for the conspicuous part he acted in the early stages of the opposition to the measures of the British Government. When 15 years of age, his father proposed to John either to follow the family pursuits, and to receive in due time his portion of the estate, or to have the expense of a learned education bestowed upon him, with which, instead of any fortune, he was to make his way in future life. He chose the latter; and having received some preparatory instruction, was admitted at Harvard College in 1751. After graduating in 1755, he removed to the town of Worcester, where, according to the economical practice of that day in New England, he became a tutor in a grammar school, and at the same time began the study of law; and was admitted to practice in 1758. In 1765 he was chosen one of the representatives of his native town to the congress of the province. His first prominent appearance in political affairs was at a meeting to oppose the Stamp Act.

The resolutions he proposed were carried unanimously, and were adopted by more than forty other towns. In 1768 he removed to Boston.

When it was determined, in 1774, to assemble a general Congress from the several Colonies, Adams was one of those selected by the people of Massachusetts. Before departing for Philadelphia to join the Congress, he parted with his fellow-student and associate at the bar, Jonathan Sewall, who had attained the rank of attorney-general, and was necessarily opposed to his political views. Sewall made an effort to change his determination, and to deter him from going to the Congress. He urged that Britain was determined on her system, and was irresistible, and would be destructive to him and all those who should persevere in opposition to her designs. To this Adams replied: "I know that Great Britain has determined on her system, and that very fact determines me on mine. You know I have been constant and uniform in opposition to her measures; the die is now cast; I have passed the Rubicon; to swim or sink, live or die, survive or perish with my country, is my unalterable determination."

When the Continental Congress assembled Adams became one of its most active and energetic leaders. He was a member of the committee which framed the Declaration of Independence; and one of the most powerful advocates for its adoption by the general body; and by his eloquence obtained the unanimous suffrages of that assembly. Jefferson said, "Mr. Adams was the Colossus on that floor." Though he was appointed chief-justice in 1776, he declined the office, in order to dedicate his talents to the general purpose of the defence of the country.

In 1777 he, with three other members, was appointed a commissioner to France. He remained in Paris nearly two years, when, in consequence of disagreements, all but Franklin were recalled. In the

JOHN ADAMS.

end of 1779 he was charged with two commissions, —one to treat for peace, the other empowering him to form a commercial treaty with Great Britain. He went to Holland, and there, in opposition to the influence and talents of the British Minister, he succeeded in negotiating a loan, and in procuring the assistance of that country in the defence against Great Britain. He formed a commercial treaty with Holland. In 1785 he was appointed Ambassador to the Court of his former Sovereign, King George III. He returned home in 1787, after devoting ten years to the public service ; received the thanks of Congress, and was elected under the Presidency of Washington, to the office of Vice-President. In framing fundamental laws and State papers, he displayed the highest qualities of a jurist and a statesman, while in his negotiations abroad he exhibited rare diplomatic sagacity. He was among the strongest and wisest of our State Builders, and no other man had such claims to be the immediate successor of Washington.

In the Presidential contest, the Democrats had one advantage over the Federalists. Their allegiance was given entirely to one man, while their opponents were divided in their regards among divers candidates. Several influential leaders in the Northern and Eastern States desired to return Alexander Hamilton; others were inclined to support John Jay; but to the greater number John Adams seemed the fittest person for filling the office. Hamilton was considered too much inclined towards England, and Jay had rendered himself unpopular by his recent treaty with Great Britain. The contest, therefore, narrowed itself into a struggle between John Adams and Thomas Jefferson. Adams enjoyed the confidence of many in the Northern States; even among the Southern, he was not entirely devoid of friends and believers; and Jefferson himself observed that he was the only sure barrier against Hamilton's getting in.

As we have seen, the election was a very close one. The votes received by Adams were 71, which was one more than the requisite number. Jefferson stood only three votes lower, and therefore became Vice-President. Although Adams was thus successful, the narrowness of his majority (and that it was a majority at all was due to a few unexpected votes from the South) showed how strong a party existed against the opinions which he embodied. He called himself "the President of *three* votes," and felt that his position was insecure, or at least extremely difficult. Yet he determined to abate not one jot in vindication of his opinions. On March 4, 1797, he took the oath of office. The ceremony was performed in the House of Representatives, but without any distinctive circumstances. In his inaugural speech, Adams made it sufficiently clear that his alleged preference for a monarchy had no foundation in fact, and it was generally admitted that his statement of principles was satisfactory. Washington was present as a spectator. Adams adopted as his own the Cabinet left by Washington. George Cabot of Massachusetts was appointed Secretary of the Navy, May 3, 1798. Naval affairs had been under the control of the Secretary of War until the Navy Department was organized, April 30, 1798.

The French Revolution now reached its highest point, and our people naturally took sides. Adams found he would have to arm to preserve neutrality and at the same time punish the aggression of either of the combatants. This was our first exhibition of "armed neutrality." A navy was quickly raised, and every preparation made for defending our rights. An alliance with France was refused, our minister was dismissed; and the French navy began to cripple our trade. In May, 1797, President Adams felt it his duty to call an extra session of Congress. The Senate approved of negotiations for reconciliation with France. They were attempted, but proved fruitless. Our envoys were informed that in order to secure peace the United States must make a loan to the French Government, and pay secret bribes to members of the Directory. These demands were resisted with just disdain; and Pinckney exclaimed, in a sentence which has since become famous, "Millions for defence, but not one cent for tribute."

In May, an army was voted. To command this force Washington was called from his retirement, and, as might have been expected of him, at once obeyed the call. He stipulated that Hamilton should be the acting Commander-in-Chief, and that the principal officers should be such as he approved; and, as on previous occasions, he declined to receive any part of the emoluments attached to the office, except as a reimbursement of sums he might himself lay out. A large part of his time, to the end of his life, was taken up with the organization of the new force which it was found necessary to create.

For the office of his Inspector-General, and his two Major-Generals, he proposed Hamilton, Charles Cotesworth Pinckney, and General Henry Knox. This arrangement displeased Knox, who believed, that as an older officer than either of the other two, he had a claim to the post of Inspector-General.

An attempt was made by some members of Congress to bring on a declaration of war; but the attempt failed. The President and his Cabinet were hopelessly at issue, and the latter omitted no opportunity of embarrassing their chief's plans. The feeling of the country was in favor of war. Adams suffered from the difficulties which naturally belong to moderation. He was not loved by either of the contending parties, since he held aloof from the exaggerations of both. He was disliked by the Democrats, because he would not be the servant of France; he was equally disliked by the Ultra-Federalists, because he declined to rush headlong into a wild crusade against the Directory and its principles. Nothing, however, was more conspicuous in Adams than strength of will. Although Congress was not heartily in his favor, and his own Cabinet were very much against him, he persevered in his views.

The friends of Hamilton, in the early summer of 1799, appealed to Washington to put himself forward once more as a candidate for the Presidential office. The idea was to some extent, though secretly, supported by the members of Adams' Cabinet; it met with great favor in the New England States; and Gouverneur Morris of New York was commissioned to address to the Commander-in-Chief a specific request to this effect. Death prevented Washington's knowing anything of the design; and it is more than likely that he would have refused to connect himself with it. He had done enough for duty, for fame, and for immortality, and it was not possible for him to stoop to the vulgar level of party intrigues.

The relations between Adams and his Cabinet grew daily more unsatisfactory. The latter were much under the influence of Hamilton, and that influence was unfavorable to the President. Adams accordingly resolved, in the early part of 1800, on changing some of them. Those who had been his confidential advisers co-operated with others to decry his character for political sagacity, and even for political honesty. Their proceedings were not unknown to Adams, who alleged that his Federal enemies were inflamed against him because he had refused to lend himself to their schemes for an alliance with England, and a war against France.

The position of the President was harassed by the alien and sedition laws, which were unpopular, and were in truth of so arbitrary a character as to furnish very good texts for the opposition to dilate upon. The Alien Act authorized the President to expel from the country any foreigner not a citizen, who might be suspected of conspiring against the Republic. The Sedition Act punished with fines and imprisonment those who might circulate "any false, scandalous, and malicious writing against the Government of the United States, or either House of Congress, or the President." The Legislatures of Virginia and Kentucky declared both these Acts to be unconstitutional, and they were eventually repealed. They were happily got rid of; though they had the approval of Washington.

The Naturalization Law was favored by the Federalists, because they knew they could acquire few friends from newly arrived English or French aliens;

among other requirements it provided that an alien must reside in the United States *fourteen years* before he could vote. The Republicans denounced this law as calculated to check immigration, and dangerous to our country in the fact that it caused too many inhabitants to owe no allegiance whatever. They also asserted, as did those who opposed Americanism later on in our history, that America was properly an asylum for all nations, and that those coming to America should freely share all the privileges and liberties of the government.

Another cause of unpopularity was found in the war-taxes imposed by Adams' Administration. We had now 16 States, and the concurrence of nine of these was necessary to a Presidential election. The official life of Adams terminated in his nominating at midnight on March 3, several of his party to high judicial functions, in accordance with a measure passed for reorganizing the Federal Courts. That Act had reduced the future number of Justices of the Supreme Court, and had increased the District Courts to twenty-three. Adams considered it necessary that these high judicial posts should be filled by members of the Federal body as a counterpoise to that reaction in favor of the Democrats which he foresaw would follow the election of Jefferson to the Presidency; but the precaution proved unavailing. Just then, Oliver Ellsworth resigned his position as Chief Justice of the Supreme Court. Adams offered the place to Jay, and, on that gentleman declining to serve, because of bad health, conferred it on John Marshall, who, not long before, had been made Secretary of State. The other appointments were conceived in the same spirit and with the same object, and Jefferson always resented them very strongly, as a check on the designs which he determined to carry out as soon as power had passed into his hands.

In the Presidential election of 1800 John Adams was the nominee for President and Charles C. Pinckney for Vice-President. A "Congressional Convention" of Republicans, held in Philadelphia, nominated Thomas Jefferson and Aaron Burr as candidates for these offices. On the election which followed, the Republicans chose 73 electors and the Federalists 65. Each elector voted for two persons, and the Republicans so voted that they unwisely gave Jefferson and Burr *each* 73 votes. Neither being highest, the election had to go to the House of Representatives for settlement. The Federalists threw 65 votes to Adams and 64 to Pinckney. The Republicans could have done the same, but Burr's intrigue and ambition prevented this, and the result was a protracted contest in the House, and one which put the country in great peril, but which plainly pointed out some of the imperfections of the electoral features of the Constitution. Jefferson was elected on the 36th ballot. The bitterness of this strife, and the dangers which similar ones threatened, led to an abandonment of the old system and an amendment was offered requiring the electors to ballot separately for President and Vice-President.

Jefferson was the first candidate nominated by a Congressional caucus. It convened in 1800 at Philadelphia, and nominated Thomas Jefferson, of

Virginia, for President, and Aaron Burr, of New York, for Vice-President. Adams and Pinckney were not nominated, but ran and were accepted as national leaders of their party, just as Washington and Adams were before them. This contest broke the power of the Federal party.

AARON BURR.

The defeat of Adams was not unexpected by him, yet it was regretted by his friends. He retired with dignity, at 68 years of age, to his native place, formed no political factions against those in power, but publicly expressed his approbation of the measures which were pursued by Jefferson. He died in Braintree, Massachusetts, July 4, 1826—the fiftieth anniversary of the Declaration of Independence—and by a singular coincidence, Jefferson, his political rival, but firmly attached friend, died a few hours earlier the same day. Adams' last words were, "Jefferson still survives;" he was not aware that Jefferson had died four hours earlier.

John Adams holds no second rank among the

founders of the Republic. In depth and breadth of comprehension; in heroic statesmanship; in fire and persuasion of eloquence; in clearness of prophetic gaze; in warm sympathies and defence of human rights; in his estimate of the dignity and sacredness of man; in his idolatrous worship of Human Liberty;. in his hatred of Despotism; in his matchless executive ability; in his broad and varied political knowledge; in the depth and clearness with which he stamped the seal of his mind and character upon the men of his time, and those who were to come after him—he has had no equal in our history.

THOMAS JEFFERSON—1801–1809.

THOMAS JEFFERSON, the third President, was born April 2, 1743, in Virginia. He was the eldest son in a family of eight children. At college he was noted for his close application to his studies. He was versed in Latin and Greek, and Italian, French and Spanish. He studied law, and was admitted to the bar in 1767, and his success in his chosen profession was remarkable. In 1769 he was a member of the Virginia House of Burgesses. He was elected in 1774 a member of the Convention to choose delegates to the first Continental Congress at Philadelphia. In June, 1775, he took his seat in the Congress; and was appointed one of a committee to draft a declaration of independence—when he produced that great State paper and charter of freedom, known as the *Declaration of Independence*, which on July 4, 1776, was unanimously adopted and signed

THOMAS JEFFERSON.

by all of the fifty-six members present, excepting John Dickinson of Pennsylvania.

The Declaration of Independence is equal to anything ever borne on parchment or expressed in the visible signs of thought. The heart of Jefferson in writing it, and of Congress in adopting it, beat for all humanity. In the Virginia Assembly he procured the repeal of the laws of entail, the abolition of primogeniture, and the restoration of the rights of conscience. These reforms he believed would do away with every fibre of ancient or future aristocracy.

In 1779 he succeeded Patrick Henry as Governor of Virginia. He declined a re-election in 1781. In 1783 he returned to Congress, where he established the present Federal system of coinage, doing away with the English pounds, shillings, and pence. In 1785 he succeeded Benjamin Franklin as Minister at Paris; and here began that attachment for the French nation which appeared in all his subsequent career. He returned to Virginia in 1789, shortly after Washington's election to the Presidency. He was immediately offered the office of Secretary of State, which he at once accepted. He disagreed with Hamilton in nearly all his financial measures, and to avoid the squabblings among the Cabinet he resigned his office December 31, 1793. At the close of Washington's second term he was brought forward as the Presidential candidate of the Republicans. John Adams, the Federalist nominee, was elected, and Jefferson receiving the next highest number of votes, was declared Vice-President. The offices were thus divided by the candidates of the two opposing parties.

The inauguration of Jefferson took place March 4, 1801. It would have been more courteous had Adams

A Declaration by the Representatives of the UNITED STATES OF AMERICA, in General Congress assembled.

When in the course of human events it becomes necessary for one people to advance from the subordination in which they have hitherto remained, & to assume among the powers of the earth the separate and equal station to which the laws of nature & of nature's god entitle them, a decent respect to the opinions of mankind requires that they should declare the causes which impel them to the separation.

We hold these truths to be self-evident: that all men are created equal & independent; that from that equal creation they derive rights inherent & inalienable; among which are the preservation of life, & liberty, & the pursuit of happiness; that to secure these ends, go-

THE FIRST DRAFT OF THE DECLARATION OF INDEPENDENCE IN JEFFERSON'S HANDWRITING, *from the original, preserved in Washington.)*

49

John Hancock

Sam¹ Adams   *Phil. Livingston*
Rob¹ Treat Paine   *Wᵐ Floyd*
John Adams   *Fran⁵ Lewis*
Elbridge Gerry
Josiah Bartlett   *Richᵈ Stockton*
Samˡ Huntington

Step. Hopkins   *John Hart*
Abra Clark   *Lewis Morris*
         John Morton
Matthew Thornton
Roger Sherman   *John Penn*
Wᵐ Whipple   *Jn⁰ Witherspoon*
William Ellery   *Wᵐ Hooper*
Oliver Wolcott   *Rob¹ Morris*
Benjⁿ Franklin   *Wᵐ Williams*
Fras. Hopkinson   *Wᵐ Paca*   *Thos. Stone*
Charles Carroll of Carrollton

50   SIGNERS OF THE DECLARATION.

[Signatures: Th Jefferson, Geo Taylor, Edward Rutledge, Joseph Hewes, Jas. Smith, Geo Ross, Geo Clymer, Thos M'Kean, Button Gwinnett, James Wilson, Geo Read, Thomas Lynch Junr, Samuel Chase, George Wythe, Benjamin Rush, Lyman Hall, Richard Henry Lee, Ths Nelson jr., Arthur Middleton, Cæsar Rodney, Carter Braxton, Benj Harrison, Geo Walton, Francis Lightfoot Lee, Thos Heyward Junr.]

SIGNERS OF THE DECLARATION.

remained at the Federal capitol until the installation of his successor; had he been present at the ceremony, and spoken some words of formal compliment. But he was a man of quick and passionate nature, and did not care to grace the spectacle of his rival's entry into power. He was irritated also by the defection of those of his own party whose treachery had caused his defeat. From these causes, the retiring President felt unable, or unwilling, to do towards Jefferson what Washington had done towards himself. He left the capitol just before the inauguration and from that time to the end of his long life ceased to have any vital influence on the course of American politics.

With the year 1801, a change took place in the policy of the Government. Jefferson, the new President, had forsaken the Northern supporters of Independence and of the existing political condition. He had founded a party, the great objects of which were to weaken the general powers of the Union, and to hold authority within the narrowest limits. To that party he had given the energy of his genius, the strength of his will, and the force and mastery of his organizing abilities. The mistakes of Adams' Presidency—mistakes for which the subordinates were more responsible than the chief—had vastly improved the position of Jefferson and his friends, and the new President found himself at the head of a numerous body of supporters, with an ever-increasing accession of opinion in most parts of the country. In the period during which he held office, he was able to give a new direction to affairs, and to create an impulse which, with but few checks or reactions, continued for sixty years.

On assuming office, Jefferson was nearly 58 years of age. He was therefore about eight years younger than his rival, and represented a somewhat more modern tone of thought. Starting on his career with the entire confidence of the Democratic party, he was regarded with proportionate distrust by the Federals; but his inaugural speech was of a nature to allay their fears. None the less was Jefferson determined to carry out those projects of reform which he conceived to be necessary to the existence of Republican institutions. Since Jefferson's time, it has been usual for Presidents, on coming into power, to effect a complete change in the Administration, and to make appointments in strict conformity with party lines. There is this to be said for this system, it is obviously easier for a man to work with his own political followers than with those who are perhaps biassed in favor of different opinions. But to Jefferson it appeared an indispensable concomitant of democratic rule. James Madison of Virginia became Secretary of State; Henry Dearborn of Massachusetts, Secretary of War; and Levi Lincoln of Massachusetts, Attorney-General. Madison, some years before, had been one of the most energetic of the Federals, but had long gone over to the opposite party. Before the end of the year, Albert Gallatin of Pennsylvania had succeeded Dexter in the Treasury, and Robert Smith of Maryland had been made Secretary of the Navy.

With little delay, Jefferson set to work reforming and retrenching. He reduced the army and navy; cut down the diplomatic corps; submitted to Congress a bill for diminishing the Judiciary; and proposed the remission of taxes. The internal or Excise duties, always unpopular, and now no longer necessary, were abolished; and this enabled the President to do away with a number of offices which had proved burdensome to the country. The paying off of the national debt was an excellent work; but it could hardly have been effected had not Hamilton already placed the finances in a healthy condition.

In 1802, a part of the North-western Territory, which had been first organized in 1787, was erected into an independent State, with the title of Ohio. The population increased with extraordinary rapidity after the large cession of Indian lands in 1795, consequent on the successful war which had been carried on by General Wayne. The sense of security thus produced caused a rush of emigration towards the North-west, and in 1802 Ohio had a population of about 72,000. The Constitution was framed in November, and by this instrument it was provided that slavery should forever be excluded from the State. In 1851 another Constitution was adopted, but the curse of negro bondage has never been admitted within the limits of this western Government.

Congress, on the recommendation of Jefferson, established a uniform system of naturalization, and so modified the law as to make the required residence of aliens five years, instead of fourteen, and to permit a declaration of intention to become a citizen at the expiration of three years. By his recommendation also was established the first sinking fund for the redemption of the public debt. It required the setting apart annually for this purpose the sum of $7,300,000. Other measures, more partisan in their character, were proposed, but Congress showed an aversion to undoing what had been wisely done. The provisional army had been disbanded, but the

ON THE BANKS OF THE MISSISSIPPI RIVER

proposition to abolish the naval department was defeated.

Now was passed the first law in relation to the slave trade. It was to prevent the importation of negroes, mulattoes, and other persons of color into any port of the United States within a State which had prohibited by law the admission of any such person. The slave trade was not then prohibited by the Constitution.

The most important occurrence under Jefferson was the purchase and admission of Louisiana. There had been fears of a war with Spain, which arose over the south-western boundary line and the right of navigating the Mississippi. Our Government learned, in the spring of 1802, that Spain had by a secret treaty, made in October, 1800, actually ceded Louisiana to France.

Bonaparte proposed that we should purchase Louisiana, and the offer was at once accepted. This immense region, watered by one of the finest rivers in the world, and conferring the command of all that part of America, was added to the United States for $15,000,000. The bargain was concluded on April 30, 1803, and we took possession on December 20th. Napoleon observed that "the new accession of territory would permanently strengthen the power of the United States, and that he had just given to England a maritime rival who would sooner or later humble her pride." It was objected by some that the Floridas and New Orleans would have been a more important acquisition than the whole of Louisiana;

to which Jefferson astutely replied that the Floridas, being now surrounded, must in time be absorbed in the Union. Not many years elapsed before his words proved true, and in the meanwhile the possession of Louisiana assured to us an immense extension westward. This very fact, however, was regarded by several as a source of danger. The Western States, it was argued, had already a considerable tendency to separate from their Eastern brethren; and, now that they were reinforced by this enormous region, would form a distinct confederation.

Little chance was afforded the Federalists for adverse criticism in Congress, for the purchase proved so popular that the people greatly increased the majority in both branches of Congress, and Jefferson called it together earlier for the purpose of ratification.

The Republicans closed their first national administration with high prestige. They had met several congressional reverses on questions where defeat proved good fortune, for the Federalists kept a watchful defence, and were not always wrong. The latter suffered numerically, and many of their best leaders had fallen in the congressional contest of 1800 and 1802, while the Republicans maintained their own additions in talent and number.

In 1804 the candidates of both parties were nominated by congressional caucuses. Jefferson and George Clinton of New York were the Republican nominees; Charles C. Pinckney and Rufus King of New York were the nominees of the Federalists, but they only received 14 out of 176 electoral votes. Burr had come too near the Presidency to be made prominent with Jefferson's consent, and so was dropped in favor of George Clinton.

During the development of these events, affairs progressed in a peaceful and orderly fashion. The President recommended an exploring expedition across the continent from the Mississippi to the Pacific, and its members, to the number of thirty, left the Mississippi on May 14, 1804. They were absent over two years, and returned laden with information which gave a clearer conception of the vast and important region lying between the great river and the Western Ocean.

One tragic incident threw a lurid stain on the political contests of 1804. A quarrel occurred between Alexander Hamilton and the Vice-President. The former had reflected upon the character of the latter in public, and had caused him to lose his election as Governor of New York. Burr demanded a retraction, which Hamilton refused. Burr challenged him, and they met. Hamilton discharged his pistol in the air, but the fire of Burr's weapon took deadly effect. The wounded man expired July 13th, and the event produced a general sense of indignation throughout the Union.

Jefferson's second term of office began March 4, 1805. His previous administration had been singularly successful. He had reduced the public debt more than twelve millions; had lessened the taxes; doubled the area of the United States by his judicious treaties with France and with the Indians; had chastised the Barbary pirates, and advanced the reputation of the country as a naval Power. The reward of these services was, that he received more

A STEAMER AT NEW ORLEANS WITH FOUR THOUSAND BALES OF COTTON ON DECK.

votes at his re-election in 1804 than at his first appointment to the Presidency in 1800.

The struggle of Napoleon in Europe with the allied Powers now gave Jefferson an opportunity to inaugurate a foreign policy. England had forbidden all trade with the French and their allies, and France had in return forbidden all commerce with England and her colonies. Both of these decrees violated our neutral rights, and were calculated to destroy our commerce, which by this time had become quite imposing.

Congress acted promptly, and passed what is known as the Embargo Act, under the inspiration of the Republican party, which claimed that the only choice of the people lay between the embargo and war, and that there was no other way to obtain redress from England and France. But the promised effects of the measure were not realized, and when dissatisfaction was manifested by the people, the Federalists made the question a political issue. Political agitation increased the discontent, and public opinion at one time turned so strongly against the law that it was openly resisted on the Eastern coast, and treated with almost as open contempt on the Canadian border.

In January, 1809, the then closing administration of Jefferson had to change front on the question, and the law was repealed.

During the Congress which assembled in December, 1805, the Republicans dropped their name and accepted that of "Democrats." In all their earlier strifes they had been charged by their opponents with desiring to run to the extremes of the democratic or "mob rule," and fear of too general a belief in the truth of the charge led them to denials and rejection of a name for which the father of their party had ever shown a fondness. From now on the Jeffersonian Republicans called themselves Democrats, and the word Republicans passed into disuse until later on in the history of our political parties, the opponents of the Democracy accepting it as a name which filled the meaning of their attitude in the politics of the country.

A resolution appropriating two million dollars for the acquisition of Florida was carried after an animated debate, but the House now attacked the policy of the Government with great vigor, and it was not until fifteen years later that Florida passed into our possession.

Public opinion was exasperated to a pitch of fury by an event which gave a more than usually irritating character to the question of the right of search. The British ship-of-war *Leopard* was cruising off Virginia. The American frigate *Chesapeake* was not far away. She was hailed, and a boat despatched with a letter to the chief officer, informing him that the English Admiral had given orders to take any British deserters from the *Chesapeake*—by force, if necessary—and at the same time to allow, on his own part, a search for deserters. Permission to search was refused. The *Leopard* thereupon fired into the *Chesapeake*, killing some of the crew; and the latter, being unprepared for action, immediately struck her flag. The English officer in command required the muster-roll of the ship, and took off four men whom he claimed as British subjects.

Rage seized on the people when the story of the *Chesapeake* came to be known. The slight resistance offered by that vessel increased the general feeling of mortification and anger. Some demanded an immediate declaration of war against England, and Jefferson observed that the country had never been in such a state since the collision at Lexington.

The commercial relations between America and the European belligerents became progressively more troublesome and vexatious. In January, 1807, Great Britain issued an order prohibiting the trade of neutrals from port to port of the French Empire. This was followed by another order forbidding neutral nations to trade with France and her allies, except on payment of tribute to Great Britain. The reply of Napoleon was a decree, issued from Milan, which declared that every neutral vessel which should submit to be visited by a British ship, or should pay the tribute demanded, would be confiscated, if afterwards found in any part of the French Empire, or if taken by any of the French cruisers. By these several orders and decrees, almost every American vessel sailing on the ocean was liable to capture. Thus we were made to suffer because England and France were at war. As a measure of protection, a law laying an indefinite embargo was enacted. The measure was passed December 22, 1807. It lasted fourteen months. It was unpopular in New England.

The embargo acted more to the disadvantage of England, as being the greatest mercantile nation in the world, than to that of France. For this very reason it enjoyed the support of the Democrats, and aroused the ire of the Federalists and of those few Democrats who had joined in the political schism created by Randolph. The feeling against England, however, arising from the antagonism of previous years, and now intensified by the persistent assertion by the British of the right of search, prevailed over every other consideration.

There was a split among the Federalists as well as among the Democrats. John Quincy Adams, son of the late President, had resigned his seat in the Senate because he differed from the majority of his constituents in supporting the measures of the Administration. He wrote to the President that it was the determination of the ruling party in New England to separate themselves from the Union if the embargo was not speedily rescinded. He gave it as his opinion that, owing to the severe pressure of the embargo upon that mercantile and trading community, they would be supported in such a course by the great body of the people, and that they were already receiving the countenance of a secret agent of Great Britain. This communication put the younger Adams on a more friendly footing with the Democratic party, and under the Presidency of Madison, he was appointed Minister to St. Petersburg. His information may in some points have been incorrect; but the Massachusetts Legislature declared the embargo ruinous at home, unsatisfactory to France, and ineffectual as a retaliation upon England.

During the discussion of these important and difficult matters, preparations were being made for the next Presidential election. Jefferson had been urged by the Legislatures of most of the Republican States to accept a third term, but he followed the patriotic example set by his predecessor, and declined. There were the two candidates of the Democratic party— Madison and Monroe—both natives of Virginia. Madison, it was known, would continue the policy of Jefferson, of whose administration he had throughout been the leading member. Monroe received the support of John Randolph, and of those seceders from the Democratic party who ranged themselves under Randolph's guidance. The choice rested with Madison, who, on the retirement of Jefferson, would be the obvious leader of the great body which his intellect and character adorned. The strength of the two candidates was tested in a caucus of the Democratic members of Congress, where a large majority declared for Madison. He was, therefore, nominated for the office of President, and George Clinton of New York for that of Vice-President. Charles C. Pinckney and Rufus King were the candidates of the Federal party; and the former received the votes of all the New England States, except Vermont, the vote of Delaware, two votes in Maryland, and three in North Carolina—making in all forty-seven votes. George Clinton received six of the nineteen votes of New York, and James Madison all the rest, amounting to 122. Madison, therefore, was the President for the ensuing four years, and Clinton retained the position of Vice-President, which he had held since 1805. Monroe received

STATUE OF JEFFERSON IN FRONT OF THE WHITE HOUSE.

scarcely any support at all, and even for the inferior office received only three votes.

Three days before Jefferson retired from office the Embargo Act was repealed.

Jefferson bade farewell to Washington March 4, 1809, and retired to his country-seat at Monticello, Virginia, and expressed a great gratification at being able to exchange the tumult of politics for the quiet of retirement.

In 1819 he took part in founding the University of Virginia, and acted as its rector till his death; which occurred on July 4, 1826, the fiftieth anniversary of our Independence. John Adams died a few hours later on that very same day. There was a grand appropriateness in the time and manner of his death, which corresponded with the greatness of his life. He lived to an extreme age, scarcely participating in any of the weaknesses which generally attend it. His mind was clear and vigorous to the last; and, as if heaven desired to give some signal token of its approval, that day of all others which they would have chosen for their departure, was heaven's choice, for Jefferson and Adams will forever divide the peculiar glories of the statesmanship of the Revolution. The following epitaph, written by himself, is inscribed on his tombstone at Monticello: "Here was buried Thomas Jefferson, Author of the Declaration of Independence, of the Statute of Virginia for Religious Freedom, and Father of the University of Virginia." He was six feet two and one-half inches high, and possessed a well-developed frame. He married in 1772; his wife bringing him a large dowry in lands and slaves; but the large and open hospitality with which he entertained friends and distinguished foreigners, left him a bankrupt at his death. He left one daughter. In religion he was a free-thinker. Slavery he considered an evil—morally and politically; in reference to it he said, "I tremble for my country when I remember that God is just." In 1848 his manuscripts were purchased by Congress, and printed.

JAMES MADISON—1809-1817.

JAMES MADISON, the fourth President, was born in Virginia, March 16, 1751; whither his father, an Englishman, had emigrated one hundred years before. He entered Princeton College, in New Jersey, in 1769, and graduated in 1771, after which he studied law. He was elected a member of the Virginia Convention in 1776, and was a member of the General Congress in 1779. From this period he was one of the most prominent men in the political history of the Republic. He was the most influential advocate of a Convention of all the States; and a delegate to that body in Philadelphia whose deliberations resulted in the abrogation of the old Articles of Confederation and the formation of the Constitution of the United States. He was regarded as the chief framer of the Constitution, and his own arduous services during eight Presidential years show how well he could interpret, in all his executive acts, the Constitution in whose handiwork he had borne so large a share.

He declined the office of Secretary of State when Jefferson resigned in 1793 under Washington's first administration, and continued to serve in Congress till 1797. He offered the Alien and Sedition laws, and was the author of the Virginia Resolutions of 1798, which protested against the attempts to increase the power of the Federal Government by forced constructions of general clauses in the Constitution. He boldly asserted the claims of the United Colonies to the Western Territory, and to the free navigation of the Mississippi River. He was appointed Secretary of State by Jefferson in 1801, and filled that office for eight years to the satisfaction of the people.

In his Cabinet he continued Robert Smith as Secretary of State until March 11, 1811, when he appointed James Monroe of Virginia to the office. Albert Gallatin was continued as Secretary of the Treasury until February 9, 1814. William Eustis of Massachusetts was Secretary of War during his first term. John Armstrong of New York, James Monroe, and William H. Crawford successively filled the office during the second term.

Madison took office at an epoch of gloom, depression and discontent. Two months earlier Massachusetts had painted the general situation in very sombre tones. "Our agriculture," they said, "is discouraged; the fisheries abandoned; navigation forbidden; our commerce at home restrained, if not annihilated; our commerce abroad cut off; our navy sold, dismantled, or degraded to the service of cutters or gunboats; the revenue extinguished; the course of justice interrupted, and the nation weakened by internal animosities and divisions, at the moment when it is unnecessarily and improvidently exposed

JAMES MADISON.

to war with Great Britain, France, and Spain." Though exaggerated by the warmth of party feeling, this statement was nearly true in the main. By the people of the North-eastern States it was greatly doubted whether matters would experience any improvement under Madison's administration, but his inaugural address had so suave and conciliatory a character, that most of his opponents were reassured and inclined to at least give him a trial. He was a man of very large political experience; his character was honorable and amiable; and having at different periods of his life been connected with both political parties, it was naturally supposed that he understood their conflicting views, and would be desirous of reconciling extreme opinions by the adoption of some middle course. Madison, however, resolved to follow the policy of Jefferson. He desired to avoid war with England, and sought by skilful diplomacy to avert the dangers presented by both France and England in their attitude with neutrals. In May, 1810, when the Non-intercourse Act had expired, Madison caused proposals to be made to both belligerents, that if either would revoke its hostile edict, the Non-intercourse Act should be revived and enforced against the other nation. This Act had been passed by Congress as a substitute for the Embargo. France quickly accepted Madison's proposal, and received the benefits of the Act, and the direct result was to increase the growing hostility of England. From this time forward the negotiations had more the character of a diplomatic contest than an attempt to maintain peace. Both countries were upon their mettle, and early in 1811, Pinckney, the American minister to Great Britain, was recalled, and a year later a formal declaration of war was made by the United States.

Just prior to this, the old issue, made by the Republicans against Hamilton's scheme for a National Bank, was revived by the fact that the charter of the bank ceased March 4, 1811, and an attempt was made to recharter it. A bill for this purpose was introduced into Congress, but postponed in the House by a vote of 65 to 64, while in the Senate it was rejected by the casting vote of the Vice-President, Clinton—this notwithstanding its provisions had been framed or approved by Gallatin, the Secretary of the Treasury. Thereupon the bank wound up its business and ceased to act. The Federalists were all strong advocates of the bank, and it was so strong that it divided some of the

HENRY CLAY.

Democrats who enjoyed a loose rein in the contest so far as the administration was concerned, the President not caring for political quarrels at a time when war was threatened with a powerful foreign nation. The views of the Federalists on this question descended to the Whigs some years later, and this fact led to the charges that the Whigs were but Federalists in disguise.

The next Congress continued the large Democratic majority, which promptly carried every administration measure, as did the following, which met November 4, 1811, Henry Clay, of Kentucky, then an ardent supporter of the policy of Madison, succeeding to the House speakership. He had previously served two short sessions in the Senate, and had acquired a high reputation as an able debater. He preferred the House at that period of life, believing his powers better calculated to win fame in the more popular representative hall.

On the quiet understanding that Madison would adopt a war policy, he was renominated for a second term. John Langdon was nominated for Vice-President, but as he declined on account of age, Elbridge Gerry, of Massachusetts, took his place. A *convention* of the opposition, representing eleven States, was held in New York City, which nominated De Witt Clinton, with Jared Ingersoll, of Pennsylvania, for Vice-President. This was the first National Convention, partisan in character, and the Federalists have the credit of originating and carrying out the idea. The election resulted in the success of Madison, who received 128 electoral votes to 89 for Clinton. De Witt Clinton was a nephew of George Clinton, Governor of New York State, and fourth Vice-President of the United States.

Though factious strife had been somewhat rife, less attention was paid to politics than to the approaching war. There were new Democratic leaders

in the lower House, and none were more prominent
than Clay of Kentucky, and Calhoun, Cheves, and

DE WITT CLINTON.

Lowndes, all of South Carolina. The policy of
Jefferson in reducing the army and navy was now
greatly deplored, and the defenceless condition in

which it left the country was the stated cause of the feuds which followed. Madison changed this policy at the earnest solicitation of Clay, Calhoun, and Lowndes, who were the recognized leaders of the war party. He had held back, hoping that diplomacy might avert a contest; but when once convinced that war was inevitable and even desirable under the circumstances, his official utterances were bold and free. He declared in a message that our flag was continually insulted on the high seas; that the right of searching American vessels for British seamen was still in practice, and that thousands of American citizens had in this way been impressed into service on foreign ships; that peaceful efforts at adjustment of the difficulties had proved abortive, and that the British ministry and British emissaries had actually been intriguing for the dismemberment of the Union.

The Act declaring war was approved by the President on June 18, 1812, and is remarkably short and comprehensive. It was drawn by William Pinckney, and was a soul-stirring message, but it did not rally all the people as it should have done. Political jealousies were very great, and the frequent defeats of the Federalists, while they tended to greatly reduce their numbers and weaken their power, seemed to strengthen their animosity, and they could see nothing good in any act of the administration.

Four Federalist representatives in Congress went so far as to issue an address opposing the war, the way in which it had been declared, and denouncing it as unjust. Some of the New England States refused to support it with their militia, and Massachusetts sent peace memorials to Congress.

A peace party was formed with a view to array the religious sentiment of the country against the war, and societies with similar objects were organized by the more radical of the Federalists.

This opposition culminated in the assembling of a convention at Hartford, at which delegates were present from all the New England States. They sat for three weeks with closed doors, and issued an address. It was charged by the Democrats that the real object of the convention was to negotiate a separate treaty of peace, on behalf of New England, with Great Britain, but this charge was as warmly denied. The exact truth has never been discovered, the fears of the participants of threatened trials for treason closing their mouths, if their professions were false. The treaty of Ghent, which was concluded on December 14, 1814, prevented other action by the Hartford Convention.

When we plunged into the 1812 War with Great Britain, our navy consisted of but twelve vessels and our army was an undisciplined body, officered by Revolutionary soldiers, too old to be efficient. On the sea we whipped her all around. Out of the 17 fights which occurred during the two years the war lasted, we won thirteen. "Don't give up the ship!" was the battle-cry of the American sailor.

On the land we did not fare so well. We made several attempts on Canada, but they all failed.

England sent over 4000 men, who took Washington

and burned the town with all its public buildings. This act of shame was done under strict orders from home. It was intended to fill us with dread of what might be expected. A second force was sent to New Orleans, where General Jackson routed them with a loss of half its men. This ended the war. Peace was made in 1815.

In February, 1815, the welcome and unexpected news of Peace reached Congress, which adjourned March 15, 1815, after repealing the Acts which had been necessary in preparing for and carrying on the war. This peace marks the final extinction of the Federalist party.

The position of New England in the war is explained by her exposed position. Such of the militia as served, endured great hardships, and they were constantly called from their homes to meet new dangers. The coast towns of Massachusetts were subjected to constant assault from the British navy, and the people felt that they were defenceless. It was on their petition that the legislature of Massachusetts finally, by a vote of 226 to 67, adopted the report favoring the calling of the Hartford Convention. These delegates were all members of the Federal party, and their suspected designs and action made the "Hartford Convention" a byword and reproach in the mouths of Democratic orators for years thereafter. It gave to the Democrats, as did the entire history of the war, the prestige of superior patriotism, and they profited by it as long as the memory of the War of 1812 was fresh. Indeed, directly after the war, all men seemed to keep in constant view the reluctance of the Federalists to support the war, and their almost open hostility to it in New England. Peace brought prosperity and plenty, but not obliv-

WILLIAM H. CRAWFORD.

ion of the old political issues, and this was the beginning of the end of the Federal party. Its decay thereafter was rapid and constant.

The next four Congresses continued Democratic. Clay had taken part in negotiating the treaty, and on his return was for the third time elected Speaker. Though 65 Federalists had been elected, but 10 votes were given to Federal candidates for Speaker, this party now showing a strong, and under the circumstances, a very natural desire to rub out party lines. The internal taxes and the postage rates were reduced.

Louisiana was admitted to the Union on April 3, 1812; and Indiana came in on December 11, 1816.

President Madison, in his message to Congress, urged a revision of the tariff, and acting on his recommendation what was at the time called a protective tariff was passed. Calhoun then supported it, while Clay proclaimed that protection must no longer be secondary to revenue, but of primary importance. The rates fixed, however, were insufficient, and our manufacturers were soon crowded out by excessive importations of foreign goods.

Peace brought with it another exchange of positions. President Madison, although he had vetoed a bill to establish a National Bank in 1815, was now (in 1816) anxious for the establishment of such an institution. Clay had also changed his views, and claimed that the experiences of the war showed the necessity for a national currency. The bill met with strong opposition from a few Democrats and nearly all of the Federalists, but it passed and was signed by the President.

A bill to promote internal improvements, advocated by Clay, was at first favored by Madison, but his mind changed and he vetoed the measure—the first of its kind passed by Congress.

When the Democrats held their caucus for the nomination of candidates to succeed Madison and Gerry, it was understood that the retiring officers and their confidential friends favored James Monroe, of Virginia. Their wishes were carried out, but not without a struggle, Wm. H. Crawford of Georgia receiving 54 votes against 65 for Monroe. The Democrats, opposed to Virginia's domination in the politics of the country, directed the effort against Monroe. Daniel D. Tompkins of New York was nominated by the Democrats for Vice-President. The Federalists named Rufus King of New York, but in the election which followed he received but 24 out of 217 electoral votes. The Federalists divided their votes for Vice-President.

Madison retired from public life on March 4, 1817, and went home to his farm, where he spent the remainder of his life. He died at Montpelier, Virginia, on June 28, 1836, aged 85 years.

JAMES MONROE—1817-1825.

JAMES MONROE, the fifth President, was born in Virginia, April 28, 1758. His earliest American ancestor was an officer in the army of Charles I, who emigrated to Virginia in 1652. It was a significant fact that the persecutions of the Non-Conformists peopled New England with the Pilgrims and Puritans; while the establishment of the Commonwealth under Cromwell drove the Cavaliers to Virginia; and to their united and harmonious efforts we owe the establishment of our Republic.

JAMES MONROE.

During the Revolutionary War, Monroe served for some time in the army, which he quitted after the battle of Monmouth, in 1778, rejoining it when his own State was invaded in 1781. He studied law under Jefferson, and when he was but 25 years old was elected a delegate to the Continental Congress. He represented us at Paris, and became Governor of his State when he returned to America. Mr. Jefferson sent him in 1802 as Envoy to France to negotiate for a right of depot on the Mississippi. But he attempted a far more important measure, for within fourteen days from his arrival in Paris, he had purchased the entire territory of Louisiana, the most important and diplomatic act in the history of this Republic.

He was inaugurated on March 4, 1817. His cabinet was composed of men of rare political distinction, even in that day of great men; yet these men were universally accepted as great without regard to their localities. Among them were John Quincy Adams, Secretary of State; William H. Crawford, Secretary of the Treasury; John C. Calhoun, Secretary of War; Benjamin Crowninshield, Secretary of the Navy; and William Wirt, Attorney-General. All were avowed Democrats, except Adams, and he had for some years forsaken the Federalists. Monroe, on his first embassy to Paris, was so strongly attached to the principles of the French Revolution that he was thought to have neglected the interests of the Government, and was recalled by Washington. On his second mission to Paris, in 1802–3, he conducted, with Livingston, the negotiations for the cession of Louisiana; and when in London, in 1806, he concluded, with William Pinckney, that treaty concerning the disputed matters between England and America which Jefferson refused to allow. He was a man of good judgment, of cautious and prudent views, and of untiring perseverance in the conduct of business; but in original genius he was inferior to his prede-

JOHN CALDWELL CALHOUN.

cessors. In character, his amiability was equal to that of Madison. He was universally respected, and his inaugural address was considered satisfactory by most sections of the country. Shortly after his accession, he made a three months' tour through a large part of the Union, passing from Maine, in the east, to Detroit, in the west. Jefferson disapproved of these progresses, as having too monarchical a character; but Washington had in practice given them his sanction.

Monroe found the manufacturing interests of the country in a very embarrassed state, owing to the competition of British goods, which, by reason of the great improvement of machinery, in England, could be much more cheaply produced there than here, and which, but for the duties it was considered necessary to impose on them, would probably have extinguished the native manufactures altogether. The industrial arts, in which we now hold so conspicuous a place, were in a very rude condition in 1817. During the colonial days of English-America, all manufactures there were not merely discountenanced, but actually forbidden, by the British Parliament. The working of iron promised at one time to be a great source of profit to the New Englanders; but it was prohibited by the Imperial Government. So also with regard to so slight a matter as the manufacture of hats: everything which could interfere with English traders was suppressed. Shortly after our Independence, attempts were made to establish manufactories of various textile fabrics; but, owing to the dearness of labor, the want of capital, and the absence of machinery, very little was effected. The imposition of the embargo at the close of 1807 was the first circumstance which gave a decided encouragement to our manufacturers. The people were compelled to fall back upon their own resources, and, notwithstanding a few failures at the beginning, considerable progress was made in a surprisingly short time. The value of native manufactured goods, as early as 1810, was $170,000,000; in 1814, it was probably $200,000,000. The exclusion of foreign commodities during the war had the natural effect of enhancing the price of those which were produced at home; and our manufacturers were beginning to drive a good trade, when the restoration of peace interfered with their prospects. The country was inundated with British and other European productions; and for some while, until legislation of a *protectionist* character came to the assistance of the native manufacturer, all industries of this kind sank considerably. From 1818, however, they revived, and thenceforward entered on a stage of progressive development.

While manufactures suffered, agriculture enjoyed a period of great prosperity. The number of persons engaged in agricultural pursuits in the year 1820 was 2,070,646; and the value of all American products (including cotton, tobacco, flour and rice), exported during the year 1823, was $37,646,000. The vast provinces of the West were being colonized by families from the Eastern States, and by emigrants from Great Britain and Ireland, who, arriving in large numbers every year, added materially to the population of the Republic, and widened the area of cultivated land. Within ten years of the peace—which brings us to about the close of Monroe's Administration—five new States had grown up in those wild domains which had only recently been hunting-grounds for the red man. England had for more than a hundred years contributed scarcely anything to the peopling of America. As America wanted what England had in excess, we were immense gainers by these large immigrations, and thenceforward made progress with amazing rapidity. In December, 1817, the Mississippi Territory was divided, and the western portion admitted into the Union as the State of Mississippi, while the eastern remained for a short time longer as a dependent province, under the title of the Alabama Territory. The latter included a portion of Georgia, which was given up for a consideration.

Monroe's first inaugural leaned toward Clay's scheme of internal improvements, but questioned its constitutionality. Clay was next to Jefferson the most original of all our statesmen and politicians. He was prolific in measures, and almost resistless in their advocacy. From a political standpoint he was the most direct author of the War of 1812, for his advocacy mainly brought it to the issue of arms, which, through him and Calhoun, were substituted for diplomacy. Calhoun then stood in broader view before the country than since. His sectional pride and bias had been rarely aroused, and, like Clay, he seemed to act for the country as an entirety.

From an early period in the century, the Spanish colonies in the South had been engaged in insurrectionary wars against the mother country, and some had succeeded in establishing their independence. It was the obvious policy of our Government to encourage these young Republics, and thus destroy the influence of Spain. Monroe very emphatically asserted the dogma that the monarchical form of government ought not to exist on this Continent—a political principle which under the designation of the "Monroe Doctrine," has been widely received from that time to the present. In his Message in 1823, he asserted the "Monroe Doctrine" in these terms: "We owe it to candor and to the amicable relations between the United States and the European Powers to declare that we should consider any attempt on their part to extend their system to any portion of this hemisphere as dangerous to our peace and safety."

In 1817 the Seminole Indians, joined by a few of the Creeks, and by some runaway negroes, began to commit depredations on the frontiers of Georgia and Alabama. General Gaines was despatched to suppress these risings, and to remove every Indian from the territory which the Creeks had ceded to the United States. He was overmatched in numbers, and General Jackson was sent to his aid. This vigorous officer raised a large force of Tennessee horsemen, in addition to the regular army, and marched into the Indian territory, which he speedily overran.

In 1819, a treaty was made by which Spain ceded us both East and West Florida, together with the adjacent islands. Florida was erected into a Territory in February, 1821, and in the following month General Jackson was appointed its first governor.

The recognition of the Spanish-American Republics by the United States followed. In 1819, the southern portion of Missouri was formed into a Territorial Government under the name of Arkansas; and in December of the same year Alabama was admitted into the Union. Early in 1820, Maine, which had for nearly 200 years been a portion of

OSCEOLA, CHIEF OF THE SEMINOLES.

Massachusetts, was severed from that State and suffered to enjoy a distinct existence as a State of our Union. Maine had originally been settled by the

INDIAN WARRIORS.

French, and was long a ground of contention between that nation and the English. The Colonial Government of Massachusetts forcibly assumed jurisdiction about 1652, and in 1677 purchased the whole province. The people of Maine, however, though as well disposed towards the Republican cause during the War of Independence as any other part of the Federation, did not approve of their connection with the State which had its capital at Boston. They desired to follow their own ways, and from 1820 downwards they have enjoyed that wish.

Missouri applied for admission to the Union, and this demand was made the occasion of a violent debate in Congress, on the vexed question of slavery. A Bill was introduced into Congress, containing a provision which forbade the existence of slavery in Missouri, when that Territory should be constituted as a State. The subject was fiercely argued during the whole session; the country caught the excitement, and the usual cry of disruption was raised. When Secession at last came, in 1861, it was no new idea: it had been threatened again and again—now by the North-east, and now by the South, according as the objects of either seemed imperilled. The division between these two great sections was strongly marked—in soil, in climate, in political institutions, in social customs, and in material interests; and the battle never raged more hotly, as far as language was concerned, than during this period. The North-eastern States, which had put an end to negro bondage among themselves, were strongly opposed to any extension of the detestable system into States about to be admitted to the Union. The South was equally desirous of widening the area of African servitude, in order that in the Senate there might be a majority of States pledged to support the custom, together with all those interests which were bound up in its existence. The Missourians themselves were inclined to go with the South; and, having refused to adopt a clause for the prohibition of slavery, the Northern States obstructed their admission into the Union. Thus the battle hung: the North taking its stand upon the cruel and immoral character of slavery; the South maintaining that, even if objectionable in itself, it was part of the existing order of things, and could not be suddenly abolished, or even curtailed, without serious danger to the whole social fabric. The slave trade had been suppressed for several years; but slaves were bred at home, and sold by one State to another. The Southern States in this way produced a good many slaves, and found a profit in disposing of them to other parts of the country. Missouri, wishing to share in these gains, violently resisted the restriction which the Northern members of Congress desired to impose, and threatened in 1819 to constitute itself a sovereign and entirely independent State, if not admitted to the Union on its own terms. The question was settled by a compromise on February 28, 1821, in accordance with which slavery was to be tolerated in Missouri, but prohibited in all other parts of the Union north and west of the northern limits of Arkansas; and upon this understanding Missouri, on August 21, 1820, was admitted to the Union as its twenty-fourth member. Such was the "Missouri Compromise," which will appear again in our history, as a source of dispute and recrimination.

This parting of the Federation into two divisions, with distinct and opposing interests, seemed to Jefferson a danger of a very menacing kind. He was not an admirer of slavery, though he did not clearly see his way to getting rid of it; and he was too wise and patriotic a citizen to desire a dissolution of the Union which he had done so much to create. He considered the proposed action of Congress, in imposing regulations on the several States with regard to the extension of slavery, as grossly unconstitutional. But the idea of a line of geographical demarcation, involving a different system of politics and morals, he feared would gather force with time, reappear again and again, and in the end produce so deadly a feeling of mutual hate that separation would become preferable to eternal discord. His anticipations were disastrously realized forty-one years later.

The year 1820 marked a period of financial distress in the country. The army was reduced, and the general expenses of the departments cut down, despite which measures of economy the Congress deemed it necessary to authorize the President to contract for a loan of $5,000,000. Distress was the cry of the day; relief the general demand. The banks failed, money vanished, instalments were coming due which could not be met, and Congress was saluted by the arrival of memorials from all the new States praying for relief to the purchaser of the public lands. The President referred to it in his Message and Congress passed a measure of relief by changing the system to cash sales instead of credit, reducing the price of the lands, and allowing present debtors to apply payments already made to portions of the land purchased, relinquishing the remainder. Applications were made at that time for the establishment of the pre-emptive system, but without effect; the new States continued to press the question and finally prevailed, so that now the pre-emptive principle has become a fixed part of our land system, permanently incorporated with it, and to the equal advantage of the settler and the Government.

During the discussion of the Missouri question, the President and Vice-President were re-elected for another term of four years. The second election of Monroe, in 1820, was accomplished *without a contest*. Out of 231 electoral votes, but one was cast against him, and that for John Quincy Adams. Mr. Tompkins, the candidate for Vice-President, was only a little less fortunate, there being 14 scattering votes against him. The Federal party was now nearly extinct. Although it still counted several members capable of making considerable opposition in Congress, it was devoid of all effective organization, and had little influence in the country generally. The policy of Monroe had been popular; his administration had been successful; and the Democrats had no difficulty in carrying him again into power. Two measures of his government were particularly well received by the people of the United States. One of these was an Act for making provision for the surviving officers and soldiers of the Revolution —an Act which was subsequently extended, so as to include the widows and children of those who had already departed; the second was an arrangement, made with Great Britain in October of the same year, by which we were allowed to share with English subjects in the fisheries of Newfoundland. It was at this period also that the boundary of the United States towards Canada, from the Lake of the Woods to the Rocky Mountains, was defined.

The remaining events of Monroe's Presidency are neither numerous nor weighty.

The revision of the tariff, with a view to the protection of home industry, and to the establishment of what was then called "The American System," was one of the large subjects before Congress at the session of 1823-24, and was the regular commencement of the heated debates on that question which afterwards ripened into a serious difficulty between the Federal Government and some of the Southern States. The Presidential election being then depending, the subject became tinctured with party politics. The protection of domestic industry not being among the powers granted, was looked for in the incidental ; and denied by the strict constructionists to be exercised for the direct purpose of protection ; but admitted by all at that time, and ever since the first Tariff Act of 1789, to be an incident to the revenue-raising power, and an incident to be regarded in the exercise of that power. Revenue the object, protection the incident, had been the rule in the earlier tariffs ; now that rule was sought to be reversed, and to make protection the object of the law, and revenue the incident. Henry Clay was the leader in the proposed revision and the champion of the American System ; he was supported in the House by many able and effective speakers, who based their arguments on the general distress then alleged to be prevalent in the country. Daniel Webster was the leading speaker on the other side, and disputed the universality of the distress which had been described; and contested the propriety of high or prohibitory duties, in the present active and intelligent state of the world, to stimulate industry and manufacturing enterprise.

The bill was carried by a close vote in both Houses. Though brought forward avowedly for the protection of domestic manufactures, it was not entirely supported on that ground; an increase of revenue being the motive with some, the public debt then being nearly ninety millions. An increased protection to the products of several States, as lead in Missiouri and Illinois, hemp in Kentucky, iron in Pennsylvania, wool in Ohio and New York, commanded many votes for the bill; and the impending Presidential election had its influence in its favor.

Two of the candidates, Adams and Clay, voted for and avowedly supported General Jackson, who voted for the bill, and was for it as tending to give a home supply of the articles necessary in time of war, and as raising revenue to pay the public debt; Crawford opposed it, and Calhoun had withdrawn as a Presidential candidate. The Southern planting States were dissatisfied, believing that the new burdens upon imports, which it imposed, fell upon the producers of the exports, and tended to enrich one section of the Union at the expense of another. The attack and support of the bill took much of a sectional aspect: Virginia, the two Carolinas, Georgia, and some others, being against it; Pennsylvania, New York, Ohio, and Kentucky being for it. Massachusetts, which up to this time had no small influence in commerce, voted, with all except one member, against it. With this sectional aspect, a tariff for protection also began to assume a political aspect, being taken under the care of the party afterwards known as Whig. The bill was approved by President Monroe; a proof that that careful and strict constructionist of the Constitution did not consider it as deprived of its revenue character by the degree of protection which it extended.

Having now filled the Presidential chair for nearly eight years, Monroe determined to follow the patriotic precedent set by Washington and Jefferson and Madison, and to retire from any further candidature.

In the election of 1824 four candidates were before the people for the office of President—General Jackson, John Quincy Adams, William H. Crawford and Henry Clay. None of them received a majority of the 261 electoral votes, and the election devolved upon the House of Representatives. John C. Calhoun had a majority of the electoral votes for the office of Vice-President, and was elected. Adams was elected President by the House of Representatives, who voted by States, from the three candidates who had the most votes, although General Jackson was the choice of the people, having received the greatest number of votes at the general election. The election of Adams was perfectly constitutional, and as such fully submitted to by the people; but it was a violation of the "voice of the people" principle; and that violation was equally rebuked. All the representatives who voted against the will of their constituents lost their favor, and disappeared from public life. The representation in the House of

Representatives was largely changed at the next election, and presented a full opposition to the new President. Mr. Adams himself was injured by it, and at the ensuing Presidential election was beaten by General Jackson more than two to one.

Clay, who took the lead in the House for Mr. Adams, and afterwards took upon himself the mission of reconciling the people to his election in a series of public speeches, was himself crippled in the effort, lost his place in the Democratic party, and joined the Whigs (then called the National Republicans). The Democratic principle was victor over the theory of the Constitution, and beneficial results ensued. It vindicated the people in their right and their power. It re-established parties upon the basis of principle, and drew anew party lines, then almost obliterated under the fusion of parties during the "era of good feeling," and the efforts of leading men to make personal parties for themselves. It showed the conservative power of our Government to lie in the people, more than in its constituted authorities. It showed that they were capable of exercising the function of self-government, and lastly, it assumed the supremacy of the Democracy for a long time. The Presidential election of 1824 is remarkable under another aspect—its results cautioned all public men against future attempts to govern Presidential elections in the House of Representatives; and it put an end to the practice of caucus nominations for the Presidency by members of Congress. They were dropped, and a different mode adopted—that of party nominations by conventions of delegates from the States.

In the spirit of pure democracy, Monroe, in retiring to his residence in Virginia, accepted the office of justice of the peace. He finally removed to the residence of his son-in-law, in New York city, where, at the age of 73, he peacefully breathed his last on the anniversary of the birth of the nation, being the third President who had departed on that memorable day. He is buried in Richmond, Virginia.

The eight years of his Presidency were known as the era of good feeling. We had conquered our enemies by land and sea, at home and abroad, and a long and glorious period of peace and prosperity had come to the young Republic. In the beginning of his first term, he visited all the Eastern and Western States. It was a proper tribute to pay to millions of men who had never seen their favorite chief; and wherever he went he was received with tokens of affectionate recognition. The sharp and angry passions of other days were allayed. He had not been elected by the triumph of a party—he was chosen to lead the nation, and he did it with the calmness, impartiality and integrity of a great and good man. Under his administration the whole country prospered.

JOHN QUINCY ADAMS—1825-1829.

JOHN QUINCY ADAMS, the sixth President, son of John Adams, the second President, was born in Massachusetts, July 11, 1767. Born while Faneuil Hall was ringing with the fiery eloquence of his father, and of Samuel Adams his relative, he breathed from his infancy the atmosphere of patriotism and statesmanship. In his eleventh year he went to France with his father, who had been sent as Minister. He went to Russia as private secretary to Chief-Justice Dana, then the American Minister. He returned home, entered Harvard College, and after graduating studied law and opened an office for its practice in Boston. In 1794 Washington appointed him Minister to the Hague. Afterwards he was elected to the Senate. When the second war with England was approaching, President Madison instructed him to leave St. Petersburg and join the other commissioners sent to negotiate the Peace Treaty at Ghent. On Monroe's accession to the Presidency, in 1817, he became his Secretary of State, which office he held when he was himself elected President.

He was inaugurated March 4, 1825. He called to his Cabinet Henry Clay as Secretary of State.

In his inaugural address, Mr. Adams observed: "Since the period of our Independence, a population of four millions has multiplied to twelve; a territory bounded by the Mississippi has been extended from sea to sea; and States have been admitted to the Union in numbers nearly equal to those of the first Federation. Treaties of peace, amity, and commerce have been concluded with the principal dominions of the earth. All the purposes of human association have been accomplished as effectually as under any other Government on the globe, and at a cost little exceeding in a whole generation the expenditure of other nations in a single year." The great parties of Federalists and Democrats, which had so long divided the country (by a conclusion more sanguine than correct) he pronounced to be extinct.

JOHN QUINCY ADAMS.

Adams was accused of having made a corrupt bargain with Henry Clay to defeat the selection of

Andrew Jackson in the House by the promise of making him his Secretary of State. This office had come to be looked upon as the stepping-stone to the Presidency. Credence was given to this accusation when Clay received his appointment. Clay angrily denied that any such bargain ever was entered into.

In his inaugural address, the chief topic was that of internal national improvement by the Federal Government. This declared policy of the administration furnished a ground of opposition against Adams, and went to the reconstruction of parties on the old line of strict, or loose, construction of the Constitution. It was clear from the beginning that the new administration was to have a settled and strong opposition, and that founded in principles of government. Men of the old school, survivors of the contest of the Adams and Jefferson times, divided accordingly—the Federalists going for Adams, the Republicans against him, with the mass of the younger generation. The Senate by a decided majority, and the House by a strong minority, were opposed to the policy of the new President.

A bill was introduced to do away with all intermediate agencies in the election of President and Vice-President and give the election to the direct vote of the people. But the amendments did not receive the requisite support of two-thirds of either the Senate or the House. This movement was not of a partisan character; it was equally supported and opposed by Senators and Representatives of both parties. Substantially the same plan was recommended later by President Jackson.

A fruitless attempt was now made to limit the President's appointing power by the Democrats trying to pass a tenure of office bill, as applicable to Government employees and office-holders; it provided, "that in all nominations made by the President to the Senate, to fill vacancies occasioned by an exercise of the President's power to remove from office, the fact of the removal shall be stated to the Senate at the same time that the nomination is made, with a statement of the reasons for which such officer may have been removed." It was also sought at the same time to amend the Constitution to prohibit the appointment of any member of Congress to any Federal office of trust or profit, during the period for which he was elected; the design being to make the members wholly independent of the Executive, and not subservient to the latter, and incapable of receiving favors in the form of bestowals of official patronage.

The tariff of 1828 is an era in our political legislation; from it the doctrine of "nullification" originated, and from that date began a serious division between the North and the South. This tariff law was projected in the interest of the woolen manufacturers, but ended by including all manufacturing interests. The passage of this measure was brought about, not because it was favored by a majority, but because of political exigencies. In the coming election, Adams, who favored the "American System," supported by Clay was opposed by General Jackson. This tariff was made an administration measure, and became an isssue in the canvass. The

New England States, which had formerly favored free trade, on account of their commercial interests, changed their policy, and, led by Webster, became advocates of the protective system. The question of protective tariff had not only become political, but sectional. The Southern States, as a section, were arrayed against the system, though prior to 1816 they favored it. In fact these tariff bills had become a regular feature in our Presidential elections, starting in 1816 and followed up in 1820-24 and now in 1828, with successive augmentations of duties; the last being often pushed as a party measure, and with the visible purpose of influencing the Presidential election. General Jackson was elected, receiving 178 electoral votes to 83 received by John Quincy Adams. John C. Calhoun of South Carolina was elected as Vice-President.

Adams retired from the Presidency, March 4, 1829. He was returned to Congress by the district in which he lived and continued to represent it for nineteen years, till his death. He died of paralysis on February 23, 1848, having been seized two days previously while attending the debates of Congress. At 80 years of age he was called "The old man eloquent." His mind was a store-house of facts. His patriotism and love of country were ardent. He lacked tact as a politician, and did not understand the sentiments and feelings of the common mind. He had no gift for winning friends, his cold manners and his disregard for the opinions of others made him enemies who succeeded in preventing his re-election.

He is buried at Quincy, Massachusetts.

ANDREW JACKSON—1829-1837.

ANDREW JACKSON, our sixth President, was born in North Carolina, March 15, 1767. He was the son of an Irishman who emigrated to this country in 1765, and died poor in 1767. His education was of the most limited kind and he showed no fondness for books. Had his parents delayed their emigration much longer, he would have lost what he called "the great privilege of being born on American soil." With an elder brother, at the age of thirteen, he joined the militia after the terrible massacre by Tarleton, and became a prisoner in 1781. After the war, and the death of his brother, he worked hard to support his mother, who had been left utterly destitute. Removing to Charleston, he studied law, and before he was 20 years old was admitted to the bar. From that time began his successful career as a lawyer in Tennessee, whither he had emigrated. In 1796 he was elected to Congress, where he served during the last year of Washington's second term. He gained so much popularity that the following year he was elected to the Senate. He left the Senate to become a judge of the Supreme Court of Tennessee. He was diverted from civil pursuits to the army, where he displayed the highest abilities as a general, both in organizing and conducting troops. The victory at New Orleans on January 8, 1815, ending in the entire defeat of the British army, completed Washington's work of freeing this country, and opened the way to the Presidency. In 1829 he became President, and was re-elected to continue his administration till

1837. With very few exceptions, no soldier or statesman has won the admiration of his country by nobler deeds, or established a fairer claim to its gratitude for his patriotism and unspotted integrity in his administration of public affairs. The people believed him to be fearless and honest; his political opponents declared he was only stupid and stubborn. Be that as it may, he acted up to his sense of duty, and no considerations could induce him to desert it.

He was inaugurated on March 4, 1829, and called John Van Buren of New York to his Cabinet as Secretary of State, where he remained only two years. He had many changes in his Cabinet. It was William L. Marcy, a Senator from New York, who used the celebrated expression, "To the victors belong the spoils," so often erroneously attributed to Jackson. Jackson believed in it, and acted upon it; he made more removals in one year than did all the other Presidents in the preceding forty years. Early in Monroe's administration, in the "era of good feeling," Jackson wrote him in these words: "Now is the time to exterminate that monster, called party spirit. By selecting [for cabinet officers] characters most conspicuous for their probity, virtue, capacity, and firmness, without regard to party, you will go far to, if not entirely, eradicate those feelings which, on former occasions, threw so many obstacles in the way of government. The chief magistrate of a great and powerful nation should never indulge in party feelings. His conduct should be liberal and disinterested; always bearing in mind that he acts for the whole and not a part of the community." With

PACKENHAM LEADING THE ATTACK ON NEW ORLEANS—DEFEATED BY JACKSON.

new times and new men the above good advice was forgotten, or possibly had to be ignored.

The election of Jackson was a triumph of democratic principle, and an assertion of the people's right to govern themselves. That principle had been violated in the Presidential election in the House of Representatives in the session of 1824-25; and the sanction, or rebuke, of that violation was a question in the whole canvass. It was also a triumph over the high protective policy, and the Federal internal improvement policy, and the loose construction of the Constitution; and of the Democracy over the Federalists, then called National Republicans; and was the re-establishment of parties on principle, according to the landmarks of the early years of the Government.

The short session of 1829-30 was rendered famous by the long and earnest debates in the Senate on the doctrine of nullification, as it was then called. It started with a proposition to limit the sales of the public lands to those then in the market, and to suspend the surveys of the public lands. The effect of such a resolution, if carried into effect, would have been to check emigration to the new States in the West, and to check the growth and settlement of these States and Territories. It was warmly opposed by Western members; and during the debate, Webster referred to the famous ordinance of 1787 for the government of the North-western Territory, and especially the anti-slavery clause which it contained.

Kentucky and Ohio were instanced as examples, and the superior improvement and population of Ohio were attributed to its exemption from the evils of slavery by Webster. This was an excitable subject, and the more so because the wounds of the

ANDREW JACKSON.

Missouri controversy, in which the North was the undisputed aggressor, were still tender. Mr. Hayne from South Carolina, representing Calhoun, the

Vice-President, answered with warmth and resented as a reflection upon the Slave States this disadvantageous comparison. This brought about the great debate, which is given in the school readers, and which we do not think it necessary to here repeat.

The President called attention to the expiration, in 1836, of the charter granted to the Bank of the United States. He doubted the constitutionality and expediency of the law creating the bank, and was opposed to a renewal of the charter. His view of the matter was that, if such an institution was deemed a necessity, it should be made a national one, in the sense of being founded on the credit of the Government and its revenues, and not a corporation independent from and not a part of the Government. The House of Representatives favored the renewal of the charter.

Thus was the "War of the Bank" begun in Congress, and in the public press; and openly at the instance of the bank itself, which set itself up as a power, and struggled for continued existence, by a demand for renewal of its charter. It allied itself to the political power opposed to the President, joined in all their schemes of protective tariff and national internal improvement, and became the head of the American system. Its moneyed and political power, numerous interested affiliations, and control over other banks and fiscal institutions, was great and extensive, and a power which was exercised and made to be felt during the struggle to such a degree that it threatened a danger to the country and the Government almost amounting to a national calamity.

The subject of renewal of the charter was agitated at every succeeding session of Congress until 1836.

In December, 1831, the National Republicans nominated candidates. Henry Clay was the candidate for the office of President, and John Sergeant for that of Vice-President. The address to the people presented the party issues which were to be settled at the ensuing election, the chief subjects being the tariff, internal improvement, removal of the Cherokee Indians, and the renewal of the United States Bank charter. Thus the bank question was fully presented as an issue in the election by that part of its friends who classed politically against Jackson. But it had also Democratic friends without whose aid the re-charter could not be got through Congress, and they labored assiduously for it.

Bitter was the contest between the President on the one side and the bank and its supporters in the Senate on the other side. The conduct of the bank produced distress throughout the country, and was so intended to coerce the President. Distress petitions flooded Congress, and the Senate even passed resolutions of censure of the President. The latter, however, held firm in his position. Webster was a Federal leader on both occasions—against the charter in 1816; for the re-charter in 1832. The bill passed the Senate after a long contest; and passed the House with little or no contest at all.

It was sent to the President, and vetoed by him July 10, 1832; the veto being based mainly on the unconstitutionality of the measure. The veto was sustained. The downfall of the bank speedily followed; it soon afterwards became a total financial wreck, and its assets and property were seized on executions. With its financial failure it vanished from public view, and public interest in it, and concern with it, died out.

The American system, and especially its prominent feature of a high protective tariff, was put in issue, in the Presidential canvass of 1832; and the friends of that system labored diligently in Congress in presenting its best points to the greatest advantage; and staking its fate upon the issue of the election. It was lost; not only by the result of the main contest, but by that of the congressional election which took place simultaneously with it. All the States dissatisfied with that system were satisfied with the view of its speedy and regular extinction, under the legislation of the approaching session of Congress, excepting only South Carolina. She held aloof from the Presidential contest, and cast her electoral vote for persons who were not candidates—doing nothing to aid Jackson's election, with whom her interests were apparently identified. On November 24, 1832, two weeks after the election which decided the fate of the tariff, that State issued an "Ordinance to nullify certain acts of the Congress of the United States, purporting to be laws laying duties and imposts on the importation of foreign commodities." It declared that Congress had exceeded its constitutional powers in imposing high and excessive duties on the theory of "protection," had unjustly discriminated in favor of one class or employment, at the expense and to the injury and oppression of other classes and individuals; that said laws were not binding on the State and its citizens;

and declared its right and purpose to enact laws to prevent the enforcement and arrest the operation of

DANIEL WEBSTER.

said acts within the limits of that State after the first day of February following. This ordinance placed the State in the attitude of forcible resistance to the laws of the United States. The ordinance of nullification was certified by the Governor of South Carolina to the President of the United States, and reached him in December. The President immediately issued a proclamation, exhorting the people of South Carolina to obey the laws of Congress; pointing out and explaining the illegality of the procedure; stating clearly and distinctly his firm determination to enforce the laws as became him as Executive, even by resort to force if necessary. He declared that "The Constitution of the United States forms a government, not a league; and whether it be formed by a compact between the States, or in any other manner, its character is the same. * * * * To say that any State may at pleasure secede from the Union, is to say that the United States are not a nation; because it would be a solecism to contend that any part of a nation might dissolve its connection with the other parts, to their injury or ruin, without committing any offence."

Bills for the reduction of the tariff were introduced, while at the same time the President, though not relaxing his efforts towards a peaceful settlement of the difficulty, made steady preparations for enforcing the law. The result of the bills offered in the two Houses of Congress was the passage of Clay's "compromise" bill on February 12, 1833, which radically changed the whole tariff system.

The President recommended the revival of some Acts, heretofore in force, to enable him to execute the laws in South Carolina; and the Senate reported such a bill. It was assailed as violent and unconstitutional, tending to civil war, and denounced as "the bloody bill"—the "force bill," etc. Webster justified the bill, both for the equity of its provisions, and the necessity for enacting them. He said that an unlawful combination threatened the integrity of the Union; that the crisis is called for a mild, temperate, forbearing, but inflexibly firm execution of the laws; and finally, that public opinion sets with an irresistible force in favor of the Union, in favor of the measures recommended by the President, and against the new doctrines which threatened the dissolution of the Union. He supported the cause of the Constitution and of the country, in the person of a President to whom he was politically opposed, whose gratitude and admiration he earned for his patriotic endeavors. The country, without distinction of party, felt the same; and the universality of the feeling was one of the grateful instances of popular applause and justice when great talents are seen exerting themselves for the good of the country. He was the colossal figure on the political stage during that eventful time; and his labors, splendid in their day, survive for the benefit of distant posterity.

In 1834 a measure was introduced for equalizing the value of gold and silver, and legalizing the tender of foreign coin, of both metals. The good effects of the bill were immediately seen. Gold began to flow into the country through all the channels of commerce, foreign and domestic; the mint was busy; and specie payment, which had been suspended in the country for thirty years, was resumed, and gold and silver became the currency of the land; inspiring confidence in all the pursuits of industry.

Agitation of the slavery question in the United States really began about this time. Congress in 1836 was flooded with petitions urging Federal interference to abolish slavery in the States; beginning with the petition of the Society of Friends of Philadelphia, urging the abolition of slavery in the District of Columbia.

Arkansas was admitted as a State into the Union, June 15, 1836, and Michigan followed on January 26, 1837.

The Presidential election of 1836 resulted in the choice of the Democratic candidate. Martin Van Buren, of New York, was elected by 170 electoral votes; his opponent, William Henry Harrison, receiving 73 electoral votes. Scattering votes were given for Webster and others. President Jackson delivered his last annual message, under circumstances exceedingly gratifying to him. The powerful opposition in Congress had been broken down, and he had the satisfaction of seeing full majorities of ardent and tried friends in each House. The country was in peace and friendship with all the world; all exciting questions quieted at home; industry in all its branches prosperous, and the revenue abundant. And as a happy sequence of this state of affairs, the Senate on March 16, 1837, expunged from their Journal the resolution, adopted three years previously, censuring the President for ordering the removal of the deposits of public money in the United States Bank. He retired from the Presidency with high honors, and died eight years afterwards at his home, the celebrated "Hermitage," in Tennessee, in full possession of all his faculties, and strong to the last in the ruling passion of his soul to sacrifice everything but honor to the glory of his native land. He is buried in Nashville, Tenn.

MARTIN VAN BUREN—1837-1841.

MARTIN VAN BUREN, our eighth President, was born at Kinderhook, in New York, December 5, 1782. All former Presidents had been direct descendants from Britons, and they had been born before the Revolution, and participated in its events. Van Buren's ancestors were Hollanders.

He was educated at the academy in his native village, studied law and was admitted to the Bar in 1803. He was distinguished neither for great learning nor eloquence; but was patient in study, and rapid in acquisition. He was ready in debate, careful to wariness in every utterance and act; sagacious as a politician, and genial in public and private life; winning friends on all sides, and retaining them by his loyalty. He took an active part in politics and was elected a State Senator in 1812. He advocated the second war against England; and voted for the protective tariff of 1828.

In 1815 he became Attorney-General of the State of New York, and in 1828 was elected its Governor. He afterwards served in the Senate; was appointed Minister to England; and in 1832 was elected Vice-President with Jackson, whose successor he became.

Though he did not win a brilliant reputation, he retired with honor.

He was inaugurated March 4, 1837, and declared his intention "to follow in the footsteps of his illustrious predecessor." He therefore caught the first full effects of the storm produced by his predecessor's financial policy, from which even Jackson's popularity and admitted honesty would hardly have saved him.

The President was scarcely settled in his new office when a financial panic struck the country with irresistible force. A general suspension of the banks, a depreciated currency, and insolvency of the Federal Treasury were at hand. The public money had been placed in the custody of the local banks, and the notes of all these banks, and of all others in the country, were received in payment of public dues. On May 10, 1837, the banks throughout the country suspended specie payments. The stoppage of the deposit banks was the stoppage of the Treasury. Non-payment by the Government was an excuse for non-payment by others. The suspension was now complete; and it was evident, and as good as admitted by those who had made it, that it was the effect of contrivance on the part of politicians and the so-called Bank of the United States (which had now become a State corporation chartered by Pennsylvania in January, 1836) for the purpose of restoring themselves to power. The promptitude with which the Bank of the United States was brought forward as a remedy for the distress showed that it had been held in reserve for that purpose; and the delight with which the Whig party saluted the general calamity, showed that they considered it their own passport to power.

Congress met in September, 1837, at the call of

MARTIN VAN BUREN.

the President, whose message was a review of the events and causes which had brought about the panic; a defence of the policy of the "specie circular," and a recommendation to break off all connection with any bank of issue in any form, looking to the establishment of an Independent Treasury, and that the Government provide for the deficit in the Treasury by the issue of Treasury notes and by withholding the deposit due to the States under the Act then in force. The message and its recommendations were violently assailed both in the Senate and House; but the measures proposed by the Executive were in substance enacted; and their passage marks an era in our financial history—making a total and complete separation of Bank and State, and firmly establishing the principle that the Government revenues should be receivable in coin only.

The next Presidential election was now at hand. The same candidates who fought the battle of 1836 were again in the field. Van Buren was the Democratic candidate. His administration had been satisfactory to his party, who commended his nomination for a second term to the different States in appointing their delegates; so that the proceedings of the convention which nominated him were entirely harmonious and formal in their nature. Richard M. Johnson, the actual Vice-President, was also nominated for Vice-President.

On the Whig ticket, William Henry Harrison of Ohio was the candidate for President, and John Tyler of Virginia for Vice-President. The leading statesmen of the Whig party were again put aside, to make way for a military man, prompted by the example in the nomination of General Jackson, the men who managed Presidential elections believing that military renown was a passport to popularity and rendered a candidate surer of election. Availability was the only ability asked for. Clay, the most prominent Whig in the country, and the acknowledged head of the party, was not deemed available; and although Clay was a candidate before the convention, the proceedings were so regulated that his

THE CAPITOL AT ALBANY, NEW YORK.

nomination was referred to a committee, ingeniously devised and directed for the purpose of preventing his nomination and securing that of General Harrison; and of producing the intended result without showing the design, and without leaving a trace behind to show what was done. The result of this secret committee balloting was: For General Scott,

16 votes; for Mr. Clay, 90 votes; for General Harrison, 148 votes. As the law of the convention impliedly required the absorption of all minorities, the 106 votes were swallowed up by the 148 votes and made to count for General Harrison, presenting him as the unanimous candidate of the convention, and the defeated candidates and all their friends were bound to loyally join in his support. And in this way the election of 1840 was effected.

The contest before the people was a long and bitter one—the severest ever known in the country up to that time. The whole Whig party and the large league of suspended banks, headed by the Bank of the United States, making its last struggle for a new national charter in the effort to elect a President friendly to it, were arrayed against the Democrats, whose hard-money policy and independent treasury schemes, met with little favor in the then depressed condition of the country. Meetings were held in every State, county, and town; the people thoroughly aroused, and every argument made in favor of the respective candidates and parties, which could possibly have any effect upon the voters. The canvass was a thorough one, and the election was carried for the Whig candidates, who received 234 electoral votes coming from 19 States. The remaining 60 electoral votes of the other 9 States, were given to the Democratic candidate; though the popular vote was not so unevenly divided; the actual figures being 1,275,611 for the Whig ticket, against 1,135,761 for the Democratic ticket. It was a complete rout of the Democratic party, but without the moral effect of victory.

In this campaign the Abolitionist, or Liberal party, nominated James G. Birney of New York and Francis Lemoyne of Pennsylvania. Their platform favored the abolition of slavery in the District of Columbia and Territories, the inter-State slave trade,

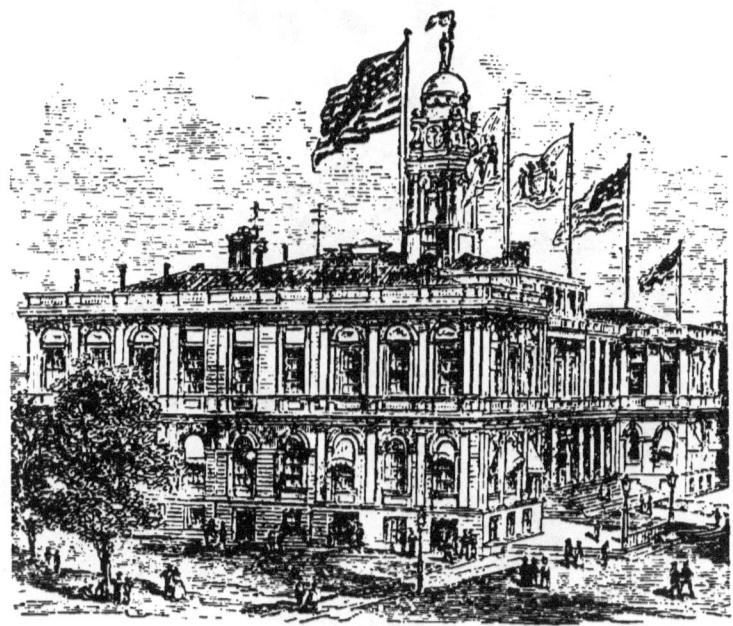

CITY HALL, NEW YORK CITY.

and a general opposition to slavery to the full extent of constitutional power. They polled 7,609 votes.

As a business man, Van Buren had no superior. He transacted business without any apparent effort or labor, and it never accumulated on his hands. In the 1844 Convention he received a majority of the votes, but owing to his objection to the annexation

GENERAL WINFIELD SCOTT.

of Texas and the adoption of the two-thirds rule, failed of a nomination. In 1848, at the solicitation of his friends, he reluctantly consented to run again when there was no hope of an election. This error of his friends defeated all future chances of success. In person he was of medium size, but became large in his old age. He was always neat in dress, and was in comfortable circumstances. On retiring from the Presidency he returned to his native town, where he died July 24, 1862.

WILLIAM HENRY HARRISON—1841 (*31 days*).

WILLIAM HENRY HARRISON, the ninth President, was born in Virginia, February 9, 1773. He was the youngest son of Governor Benjamin Harrison, a signer of the Declaration of Independence, and had the advantages of education, culture, patriotic souvenirs and early acquaintance with the scenes of frontier life. At nineteen he joined the army and served in the campaigns against the Western Indians. His command of Fort Washington, where Cincinnati now stands, secured for him in 1797 the secretaryship of the territory north-west of the Ohio, of which he was three years later chosen Delegate to Congress. In 1801 on the division of the Territory, he was appointed Governor of that portion which now embraces Indiana, Illinois, Michigan, and Wisconsin. That vast tract was held by Indians, whose ferocities were restrained by treaties till they were inflamed by Tecumseh, when Harrison advanced victoriously against them in 1811 at Tippecanoe.

The 1812 War with England now came on and

Tecumseh entered the British service and the Indians became more hostile than ever. Perry's vic-

WILLIAM HENRY HARRISON.

tory on Lake Erie enabled Harrison to drive the British and their savage allies across the line into Canada, where they were totally routed, covering the victorious general with a glory which finally carried him to the Presidency. After years of civil service he was elected, in 1824, to the United States Senate. Retiring to his farm on the Ohio for twelve years, his services having made him the most popular citizen of the Great West, he was nominated to the Presidency, and a wave of popular enthusiasm secured his triumph. The friends of Van Buren attempted to cast upon his rival the most un-American slurs. They accused him of living in a log-cabin; with nothing to drink but hard cider. Borrowing these emblems from their enemies, they became the watchword of the Whigs, and everywhere log-cabins sprang up as if by magic, and hard cider became the popular drink. Harrison was inaugurated March 4, 1841, being the first President who was not a Democrat, since Jackson's installation in 1829. To his Cabinet he called some of the most famous men of the party, and it was greeted with inspiring auguries. He was the oldest of our Presidents, and the infirmities of age led to physical prostration under the pressure of the new situation, and in one short month he was borne to his grave, leaving for himself a cherished memory and an honorable fame. He died April 4, 1841; and was buried at North Bend, Ohio.

JOHN TYLER—1841-1845.

JOHN TYLER, the tenth President, reached the Presidency through the death of General Harrison who had been in office but one month. This was the first time in the history of our Government the Vice-President had become President under the Constitution. He was inaugurated April 6, 1841; and his administration was crowded with extraordinary events.

President Tyler was born in Virginia, March 29, 1790. His father was Governor of Virginia from 1808 till 1811. At the age of twelve he was fully prepared to enter William and Mary College, from whence he graduated in 1806. He served in the Legislature for several years till 1816, when, at the age of 26, he was elected to Congress. At the close of his second term he was elected Governor of his State, whence he was advanced to the Senate. He voted for the censure on Jackson's conduct in Florida; opposed the U. S. Bank, the protective policy, and internal improvements by the National Government; opposed the administration of Adams and the Tariff Bill of 1828; sympathized with the nullification measures of South Carolina and was the only Senator who voted against the Force Bill for the repression of that incipient secession; voted for Clay's Compromise Bill, and his resolutions censuring Jackson for the removal of the deposits, although he believed the Bank unconstitutional; was regarded as a martyr to the Whig cause, and consequently supported by many of them in the campaign of 1836 for the Vice-Presidency, but was then defeated. He retained Harrison's Cabinet in office; and was expected to approve whatever a Whig Congress should do. His first message confirmed this expectation. Bills were reported for repealing the Independent Treasury, for chartering a bank, for distributing the proceeds of land-sales, and an insolvent law, under the name of a Bankrupt Act, and all were passed

JOHN TYLER.

by Congress. The Bank Act was alone vetoed by Tyler, who objected to some of its provisions. A second bill, with these modified, was passed; but this was also vetoed. This created a breach between the President and the Whigs who had elected him. A third bill was reported, but never acted upon.

A Tariff Bill, fixing the rate of duties at twenty per cent. and regulating the free list, was passed and approved. This special session pleased neither party. The Whigs carried three measures; and the Democrats rejoiced at the defeat of the Bank Bill. Both parties had their complaints. At the very next session the Bankrupt Law and the Distribution Act were repealed by the Congress that enacted them; and in 1846 the Independent Treasury Act was re-enacted, and still remains, subject to such changes as were made by Secretary Chase in 1862.

The chief measure of the Whig party—the one for which it had labored for ten years—was the recharter of a national bank. Without this all other measures would be deemed to be incomplete, and the victorious election itself but little better than a defeat. The President had been opposed to the Bank; and to overcome any objections he might have, the bill was studiously contrived to avoid the President's objections, and save his consistency—a point upon which he was exceedingly sensitive. The Democratic members resisted strenuously, in order to make the measure odious, but successful resistance was impossible. It passed both Houses by a close vote; and contrary to all expectation the President vetoed the act, falling back upon his early opinions against the constitutionality of a national bank, so often and so publicly expressed.

The vote was taken on the bill over again, as required by the Constitution, and it received only a bare majority, and was returned to the House with a message stating the objection to it, where it gave rise to some violent speaking, more directed to the personal conduct of the President than to the objections to the bill stated in his message. The veto was sustained; and so ended the second attempt to resuscitate the Bank under a new name.

The conduct of the President in the vetoes of the two bank bills produced revolt against him in the party; and the Whigs in Congress held several meetings to consider what they should do in the new condition of affairs. The rejection of the bank bill gave great vexation to one side, and equal exultation to the other. The subject was not permitted to rest, however; a national bank was the life—the vital principle of the Whig party, without which it could not live as a party; it was the lever which was to give them power and the political and financial control of the Union. A second attempt was made, four days after the veto, to accomplish the end by amendments to a bill relating to the currency, which had been introduced early in the session. The bill was pushed to a vote with astonishing rapidity, and passed by a decided majority. Concurred in by the Senate without alteration, it was returned to the House, and thence referred to the President for his approval or disapproval. It was disapproved * * * * The Whig party recoiled from the President, and there was diversity and widespread dissension. The Whig party remained with Clay; Webster retired, Cushing was sent on a foreign mission, and the President, seeking to enter the Democratic ranks, was refused by them, and left to seek consolation in privacy for his political errors and omissions.

The extra session, called by Harrison, held under Tyler, dominated by Clay, commenced May 31st, and ended September 13, 1841—and was replete with disappointed calculations, and nearly barren of permanent results. The purposes for which it was called into being failed.

In March, 1842, Henry Clay resigned his place in the Senate. He had intended this step at the close of the previous presidential campaign, but postponed it to take charge of the measures to be brought before Congress at the special session—the calling of which he foresaw would be necessary.

Mr. Clay led a great party, and for a long time. It was surprising that, without power and patronage, he was able so long and so undividedly to keep so great a party together, and lead it so unresistingly. He had great talents, but not equal to some whom he led. He had eloquence superior in popular effect, but not equal in high oratory to that of some others. But his temperament was fervid, his will was strong, and his courage daring; and these qualities, added to his talents, gave him the lead and supremacy in his party, where he was always dominant.

Again was the subject of the tariff considered, but this time, as a matter of absolute necessity, to provide a revenue. Never before were the coffers and the credit of the Treasury at so low an ebb. A deficit of fourteen millions in the Treasury—a total inability to borrow, either at home or abroad, the amount of the loan of twelve millions authorized the year before —the Treasury notes below par, and the revenues from imports inadequate and decreasing.

The compromise act of 1833 in reducing the duties gradually through nine years, to a fixed low rate; the act of 1837 in distributing the surplus revenue; and the continual and continued distribution of the land revenue, had brought about this condition of things. The remedy was sought in a bill increasing the tariff, and suspending the land revenue distribution. Two such bills were passed in a single month, and both vetoed by the President. The bill was finally passed raising the duties above twenty per cent., and approved by the President.

The next meeting of Congress showed serious losses in the Whig following. A Democratic Speaker of the House was elected. The President's message referred to the treaty lately concluded with Great Britain relative to the north-western territory extending to the Columbia river, including Oregon and settling the boundary lines; and also to a treaty with Texas for her annexation; and recommending the establishment of a paper currency to be issued and controlled by the government.

It became evident to leading Democrats that Martin Van Buren was the choice of the party. To overcome this popular current and turn the tide in favor of Calhoun, resort was had to the pending question of the annexation of Texas. Van Buren was known to be against it, and Calhoun for it. To gain time, the meeting of the convention was postponed, and when it met, consisted of 266 delegates, a decided majority of whom were for Van Buren and cast their votes accordingly on the first ballot. But a chairman had been selected who was adverse to his nomination; and aided by a rule adopted by the convention, which required a concurrence of two-thirds to effect a nomination, the opponents of Van Buren were able to accomplish his defeat. Calhoun had made known his determination not to suffer his name to go before that assemblage as a candidate for the Presidency; his reasons for so doing resting on the manner in which the convention was constituted; he contending for district elections, and the delegates to vote individually. South Carolina was not represented in the convention. After the first ballot Van Buren's vote sensibly decreased, until finally, James K. Polk, who was a candidate for the Vice-Presidency, was brought forward and nominated for the chief office. Geo. M. Dallas was chosen for the Vice-Presidency. The nomination of these gentlemen was a surprise to the country.

The Whig convention nominated Henry Clay for President, and Theodore Frelinghuysen for Vice-President.

The issues in the election which ensued were mainly the party ones of Whig and Democratic, modified by the tariff and Texas questions. It resulted in the choice of the Democratic candidates, who received 170 electoral votes as against 105 for their opponents; the popular majority for the Democrats being 238,284, in a total vote of 2,834,108. Clay received a larger popular vote than had been given at the previous election for the Whig candidate, showing that he would have been elected had he then been the nominee of his party; though the popular vote at this election was largely increased over that of 1840. It is conceded that the 36 electoral votes of New York State gave the election to Polk. Polk carried New York by about 5,000 votes. Harrison and Tyler's majority was 12,000. The "Liberty" party ran James G. Birney as a sort of test of strength, but it cost Clay the State. The great issue was the annexation of Texas. In New York the Abolitionists were as much opposed to the annexation as were the Whigs, and yet Birney polled 15,000 votes that would otherwise have gone to Clay and given him the electoral vote of the State and elected him President. Notwithstanding the party triumph, there was scarcely a Democrat there who did not feel a passing pang, at least, that "Harry of the West," "The Mill Boy of the Slashes," and the great Senator worthy of the palmy days of ancient Rome, had been defeated. It was a cruel blow of Fate, in her severest mood.

Tyler's last message contained an elaborate paragraph on the subject of Texas and Mexico; the idea being the annexation of the former to the Union, and the assumption of her causes of grievance against the latter; and a treaty was pending to accomplish these objects. Before the end of May, a great meeting took place in South Carolina to combine the slave States in a convention to unite the Southern States to Texas, if Texas should not be received into the Union; and to invite the President to convene Congress to arrange the terms of the dissolution of the Union if the rejection of the annexation should be persevered in. Responsive resolutions were adopted in several States. The opposition manifested brought the movement to a stand, and suppressed the disunion scheme for the time being.

Annexation was supported by all the power of the administration, but failed; it was rejected in the Senate by a two-thirds vote against it. Following this, a joint resolution was brought into the House for the admission of Texas as a State of the Union, by legislative action; it passed the House by a fair majority, but met with opposition in the Senate unless coupled with a proviso for negotiation and treaty, as a condition precedent, and in this shape it was agreed to, and became a law March 3, 1845. Texas was then at war with Mexico, though an armistice had been agreed upon, looking to a treaty of peace.

It has been charged that Tyler saw that Clay would be nominated as his successor, and felt stung by his overbearing and dictatorial course, and he therefore sought, by his peculiar course, to build up a separate party for himself, hoping to be made his own successor. If he entertained such views, he was sorely disappointed in the result. His course was such as to satisfy neither party. Instead of rising politically, Tyler sank down, and had few supporters in Congress and fewer elsewhere, except those in office.

Personally, Tyler possessed many good qualities. He was benevolent, kind, and warm-hearted, and without greediness for money, or a disposition to trench upon the rights of others. He possessed some qualities that unfitted him for the Presidency. He was careless, indolent, easily persuaded to anything, where old Virginia doctrines did not point out the contrary way. He was not prompt nor firm like those governed by inflexible principles. If Virginia had fully settled the question, he was ready to conform to it, but even then he was not always firm and immovable, but often drifted. On other questions he was apt to follow the course of an easy mind. The natural promptings of his mind were such as mankind could approve. The errors came in when he attempted to control his natural impulses and yield to those of selfish calculation. The attempt to limit him in the enjoyment of privileges which had been permitted all other Presidents has left more salutary enactments on the statute-book than were made in the same length of time since the repeal of the Alien and Sedition laws. He retired from office execrated by all parties. He went with the secessionists, and was a secession member of Congress when he died, showing that he had outlived all the Whigism that he once had. He died at Richmond, Virginia, January 17, 1862.

JAMES K. POLK—1845-1849.

JAMES K. POLK, the eleventh President, was born in North Carolina on November 2, 1795. His immediate ancestors emigrated from Ireland. His father removed in 1806 to Tennessee. Graduating from the University of North Carolina in 1818, he studied law, and was admitted to the bar in 1820.

He was elected to the State Legislature in 1823, and to Congress in 1825, where he continued fourteen

JAMES K. POLK.

years; and from 1835 to 1839 was Speaker of the House. He was elected Governor of Tennessee in

1839, and in 1844 he was elected President by a small majority over Henry Clay. He had always been an ardent Democrat. He became distinguished as a well-informed statesman in his opposition to John Quincy Adams, and was leader in the House during Jackson's Administration. His incorruptibility was proverbial, and his enemies never questioned his truthfulness or integrity. He sought to be right, and when he believed he was so, nothing could turn him.

He was inaugurated March 4, 1845, and called able men to his Cabinet. James Buchanan of Pennsylvania was appointed Secretary of State; Robert J. Walker of Mississippi was made Secretary of the Treasury; William L. Marcy of New York assumed the War portfolio; and George Bancroft, the historian, was selected for Secretary of the Navy.

The House was largely Democratic. At this session the "American" party—a new political organization—first made its appearance in the national councils, having elected six members of the House, four from New York and two from Pennsylvania. The President's first message had for its chief topic the admission of Texas, then accomplished, and the consequent dissatisfaction of Mexico; and a recommendation for a revision of the tariff, with a view to revenue as the object, with protection to home industry as the incident.

Florida and Iowa were admitted into the Union; the former permitting slavery within its borders, the latter denying it. Long before this, the free and the slave States were equal in number, and the practice had grown up—from a feeling of jealously and policy to keep them evenly balanced—of admitting one

State of each character at the same time. Numerically the free and the slave States were thus kept even: in political power a vast inequality was going on—the increase of population being so much greater in the northern than in the southern region.

Attempts were made in 1842, and continued to 1846, to settle the north-western boundary line with Great Britain. It had been assumed that we had a dividing line, made by previous treaty, along the parallel of 54 degrees 40 minutes from the sea to the Rocky Mountains. The subject so much absorbed public attention, that the Democratic Convention of 1844 in its platform declared for that boundary line, or war as the consequence. It became known as the 54–40 plank, and was a canon of political faith. The President had declared in his inaugural address in favor of the 54–40 line; and he was in a dilemma. To maintain that position meant war with Great Britain; to recede from it seemed impossible. Congress had come together under the loud cry of war, in which Lewis Cass was the leader, but followed by the body of the Democracy, and backed and cheered by the whole Democratic newspaper press. Under the authority and order of Congress notice had been served on Great Britain, which was to abrogate the joint occupation of the country by the citizens of the two powers. It was finally resolved by the British Government to propose the line of 49 degrees, continuing to the ocean, as originally offered by Calhoun; and though the President was favorable to its acceptance, he could not, consistently with his previous acts, accept and make a treaty on that basis. Lord Ashburton, who when there was no hope of an election. This error of his friends defeated all future chances of success. In person he was of medium size, but became large in his old age. He was always neat in dress, and was in comfortable circumstances. On retiring from the Presidency he returned to his native town, where he died July 24, 1862.

WILLIAM HENRY HARRISON—1841 (*31 days*).

WILLIAM HENRY HARRISON, the ninth President, was born in Virginia, February 9, 1773. He was the youngest son of Governor Benjamin Harrison, a signer of the Declaration of Independence, and had the advantages of education, culture, patriotic souvenirs and early acquaintance with the scenes of frontier life. At nineteen he joined the army and served in the campaigns against the Western Indians. His command of Fort Washington, where Cincinnati now stands, secured for him in 1797 the secretaryship of the territory north-west of the Ohio, of which he was three years later chosen Delegate to Congress. In 1801 on the division of the Territory, he was appointed Governor of that portion which now embraces Indiana, Illinois, Michigan, and Wisconsin. That vast tract was held by Indians, whose ferocities were restrained by treaties till they were inflamed by Tecumseh, when Harrison advanced victoriously against them in 1811 at Tippecanoe.

The 1812 War with England now came on and

Tecumseh entered the British service and the Indians became more hostile than ever. Perry's vic-

WILLIAM HENRY HARRISON.

tory on Lake Erie enabled Harrison to drive the British and their savage allies across the line into Canada, where they were totally routed, covering

had charge of the English interests, was a very keen and wily diplomatist. He met the Democratic clamor for "54–40 or fight" by saying to Calhoun and the Senate slave-holding oligarchy that in the event of a war we would undoubtedly take Canada, which would confer on the North such a political preponderance that the South would be overruled thereafter in Congress, and crushed in any disturbance she might initiate—the Canadian feeling being as pronounced against slavery as was that in the North and East. This settled the boundary question in a jiffy.

The President's Message to the next Congress related to the war with Mexico, which had been declared by almost a unanimous vote in Congress. Calhoun spoke against the declaration in the Senate, but did not vote upon it. He was sincerely opposed to the war, although his conduct had produced it. Had he remained in the Cabinet, to do which he had not concealed his wish, he would, no doubt, have labored earnestly to have prevented it. Many administration members of Congress were averse to the war. There was an impression that it could not last above three months.

While this matter was pending in Congress, Mr. Wilmot of Pennsylvania introduced and moved a proviso, "*that no part of the territory to be acquired should be open to the introduction of slavery.*" It was entirely unnecessary, as the only territory to be acquired was that of New Mexico and California, where slavery was already prohibited by the Mexican laws and constitution. The proviso only served to bring a slavery agitation on again.

The Congress, in December, 1837, was found, so far as respected the House, to be politically adverse to the administration. The Whigs were in the majority and elected the Speaker. The President's Message contained a full report of the progress of the war with Mexico; the success of the American arms in that conflict; the victory of Cerro Gordo, and the capture of the City of Mexico; and that negotiations were then pending for a treaty of peace. The message concluded with a reference to the excellent results from the independent Treasury system.

The war with Mexico was ended by the signing of a treaty of peace, in February, 1848, by the terms of which New Mexico and Upper California were ceded to the United States, and the lower Rio Grande, from its mouth to El Paso, taken for the boundary of Texas. For the territory thus acquired, the United States agreed to pay to Mexico the sum of $15,000,000, in five annual installments. The victories achieved by the American commanders—Zachary Taylor and Winfield Scott—during that war, won for them national reputation, by means of which they were brought prominently forward for the Presidential succession.

The question of the power of Congress to legislate on the subject of slavery in the Territories was again raised, on the bill for the establishment of the Oregon territorial government.

Calhoun, in the Senate, declared that the exclusion of slavery from any Territory was a subversion of the Union; openly proclaimed the strife between the North and South to be ended, and the separation of the States accomplished. "The South," he said, "has now a most solemn obligation to perform—to herself—to the Constitution—to the Union. She is

LEWIS CASS.

bound to come to a decision not to permit this to go on any further, but to show that, dearly as she prizes the Union, there are questions which she regards as of greater importance than the Union. This is not a question of territorial government, but a question involving the continuance of the Union." The President, in approving the Oregon Bill, took occasion to send in a special Message, pointing out the danger to the Union from the progress of the slavery agitation, and urged an adherence to the principles of the ordinance of 1787—the terms of the Missouri Compromise of 1820—as also that involved and declared in the Texas case in 1845, as the means of averting that danger.

The Presidential election of 1848 was coming on. The Democratic Convention met in May. The main question of the platform was the doctrine advanced by the Southern members of non-interference with slavery in the States or in the Territories. The candidates of the party were: Lewis Cass of Michigan for President, and William O. Butler of Kentucky for Vice-President.

The Whig Convention, taking advantage of the popularity of Zachary Taylor for his military achievements in the Mexican War, then just ended, and his consequent availability as a candidate, nominated him for the Presidency, over Clay, Webster, and General Scott, who were his competitors before the convention. Millard Fillmore was selected as the Vice-Presidential candidate.

A third convention was held, consisting of the disaffected Democrats from New York. They met and nominated Martin Van Buren for President, and Charles Francis Adams for Vice-President. The principles of its platform were: That Congress should abolish slavery wherever it constitutionally had the power to do so—[which was intended to apply to the District of Columbia]—that it should not interfere with it in the slave States—and that it should prohibit it in the Territories. This party became known as "Free-soilers," from their doctrines thus enumerated, and their party cry of "free soil, free speech, free labor, free men." The result of the election, as had been foreseen, was to lose New York State to the regular candidate, and give it to the Whigs, who were triumphant in the reception of 163 electoral votes for their candidates, against 127 for the Democrats; and none for the Free-soilers.

In his last Message Polk urged upon Congress the necessity for some measure to quiet the slavery agitation, and he recommended the extension of the Missouri Compromise line to the Pacific Ocean, passing through the new Territories of California and New Mexico, as a fair adjustment, to meet as far as possible the views of all parties. The President referred also to the state of the finances; the excellent condition of the public Treasury; Government loans commanding a high premium; gold and silver the established currency; and the business interests of the country in a prosperous condition. And this was the state of affairs only one year after emergency from a foreign war.

Although Polk could not rank among the great statesmen who had preceded him in that high office, yet his administration was made memorable by important events which reflected lustre upon it. He was wise in the choice of his counsellors, and fortunate in their acts. The north-western boundary question was settled. Texas had been admitted, and the war with Mexico, which followed, was conducted with so much energy and success in the field, and the great ability of Marcy in the Cabinet, that the acquisition of a vast territory from Mexico, the immediate discovery of gold in California, and the impulse thus given to the advance in population to the Pacific, all combined to render the administration of Polk a most memorable one in our history. Taken altogether, it realized what the old Federalists used to call "Jefferson's day-dreams." In the light of later events too much praise cannot be awarded to him for the distinct announcement, in the beginning of his term, that under no circumstances would he allow himself to be considered a candidate a second time. He retired from office March 4, 1849, and died at Nashville, June 15, 1849.

ZACHARY TAYLOR—1849-1850.

GENERAL ZACHARY TAYLOR, our twelfth President, was born in Virginia, in 1784. His father was a colonel in the Continental Army and fought by the side of Washington. He entered the army in 1808, and rose by regular gradations to be a major-general. He was engaged in fights with the Indians and brought the Seminole War to a close. His successes in the Mexican War gave him so much public favor that the Whigs nominated him for President in 1848, and elected him over Lewis Cass. Millard Fillmore, of New York, was elected with him as Vice-President.

He was inaugurated March 4, 1849. He chose a very able Cabinet, selecting all Whigs; although

ZACHARY TAYLOR.

from the gate of the capitol he announced his intention of conducting his administration on the principles of the early Presidents—that he would be President of the nation and not of a party. He knew his want of qualifications for civil office; and frequently expressed his regret that he ever consented to run for the Presidency, saying that "Mr. Clay ought to have been in his place." He was 65 years old when inaugurated and he was a confiding man and freely trusted his friends. He was but sixteen months in office, dying in Washington, July 9, 1850. He was buried at Louisville, Kentucky.

His death was a public calamity. No man could have been more devoted to the Union nor more opposed to the slavery agitation; and his position as a Southern man and a slaveholder—his military reputation, and his election by a majority of the people as well as of the States, would have given him a power in the settlement of the pending questions of the day which no President without these qualifications could have possessed.

In accordance with the Constitution, the office of President thus devolved upon the Vice-President, Millard Fillmore, who was duly inaugurated July 10, 1850. A new Cabinet, with Daniel Webster as Secretary of State, was appointed and confirmed by the Senate.

Congress met in December, 1849. The Senate consisted of sixty members, among whom were Webster, Calhoun, and Clay, who had returned to public life. The House had 230 members; and although the Whigs had a small majority, the House was so divided on the slavery question in its various phases, that the election for Speaker resulted in the choice of the Democratic candidate, Cobb, of Georgia, by

GENERAL TAYLOR AT BUENA VISTA, MEXICO.

147

a majority of three votes. President Taylor's Message plainly showed that he comprehended the dangers to the Union from a continuance of sectional feeling on the slavery question, and he averred his determination to stand by the Union to the full extent of his obligations and powers. Congress had spent six months in endeavoring to frame a satisfactory bill providing territorial governments for California and New Mexico, and had adjourned without accomplishing it, in consequence of inability to agree upon whether the Missouri Compromise line should be carried to the ocean, or the Territories be permitted to remain as they were—slavery prohibited under the laws of Mexico. Calhoun brought forward, in the debate, a new doctrine—extending the Constitution to the Territory, and arguing that as that instrument recognized the existence of slavery, the settlers in such Territory should be permitted to hold their slave property taken there, and be protected. Webster's answer to this was that the Constitution was made for States, not Territories; that it cannot operate anywhere, not even in the States for which it was made, without acts of Congress to enforce it. The proposed extension of the Constitution to Territories, with a view to the transportation of slavery along with it, was futile and nugatory without the Act of Congress to vitalize slavery under it.

The early part of the year had witnessed ominous movements—nightly meeting of members from the slave States, led by Calhoun, to consider the state of things between the North and the South. They prepared an address to the people. It was in this condition of things, that President Taylor expressed his opinion, in his Message, of the remedies required. California, New Mexico and Utah, had been left without governments. For California, he recommended that having a sufficient population and having framed a Constitution, she be admitted as a State into the Union; and for New Mexico and Utah, without mixing the slavery question with their territorial governments, they be left to ripen into States, and settle the slavery question for themselves in their State Constitutions.

With a view to meet the wishes of all parties, Clay introduced compromise resolutions providing for the admission of California—the territorial government for Utah and New Mexico—the settlement of the Texas boundary—slavery in the District of Columbia—and for a fugitive slave law. It was earnestly opposed by many, as being a concession to the spirit of disunion—a capitulation under threat of secession; and as likely to become the source of more contentions than it proposed to quiet.

Jefferson Davis, of Mississippi, afterwards President of the Southern Confederacy, objected that the measure gave nothing to the South in the settlement of the question; and he required the extension of the Missouri Compromise line to the Pacific Ocean as the least that he would be willing to take, with the specific recognition of the right to hold slaves in the Territories below that line; and that, before such Territories are admitted into the Union as States, slaves may be taken there from any of the United States at the option of their owner.

Clay in reply said: " Coming from a slave State,

as I do, I owe it to myself, I owe it to truth, I owe it to the subject, to say that no earthly power could induce me to vote for a specific measure for the introduction of slavery where it had not before existed, either south or north of that line. * * * If the citizens of those Territories choose to establish slavery, I am for admitting them with such provisions in their Constitutions; but then it will be their own work, and not ours, and their posterity will have to reproach them, and not us, for forming Constitutions allowing the institution of slavery to exist among them."

Following this, Calhoun said, "All the elements in favor of agitation are stronger now than they were in 1835, when it first commenced, while all the elements of influence on the part of the South are weaker. Unless something decisive is done, what is to stop this agitation, before the great and final object at which it aims—the abolition of slavery in the States—is consummated? If something decisive is not now done to arrest it, the South will be forced to choose between abolition and secession."

Calhoun died in the spring of 1850, before the separate bill for the admission of California was taken up. His death, at 68, took place at Washington. He was the first great advocate of the doctrine of secession. He was the author of the nullification doctrine, and an advocate of the extreme doctrine of State Rights. He was an eloquent speaker—a man of strong intellect. His speeches were plain, strong, concise, sometimes impassioned, and always severe. Daniel Webster said of him, that "he had the basis, the indispensable basis of all high characters, and that was, unspotted integrity, unimpeached honor and character!"

The bill to admit California was called up in the Senate and sought to be amended by extending the Missouri Compromise line through it, to the Pacific Ocean, so as to authorize slavery in the State below that line. The amendment was pressed by Southern friends of the late Mr. Calhoun, and made a test question. It was lost, and the bill passed by a two-third vote. The bill went to the House of Representatives, was readily passed, and promptly approved by the President. Thus was virtually accomplished the abrogation of the Missouri Compromise line; and the extension or non-extension of slavery was then made to form a foundation for future political parties.

MILLARD FILLMORE—1850–1853.

MILLARD FILLMORE, the thirteenth President, was born in New York, January 7, 1800. His great grandfather was born in New England nearly 200 years ago. His own father removed to Western New York. He received very little education during his boyhood. He learned the occupation of a clothier in his youth, but when 19 he resolved to become a lawyer. His abilities, energy, and industry were equal to the undertaking. He was not quick, but prepared his cases with care and judgment. In 1828 he was elected to the Legislature and was twice re-elected. In 1832 he went to Congress as an anti-

Jackson man; where he served six years. In 1841 he was Chairman of the Ways and Means Committee, where he gained the reputation that led to his nomination as Vice-President. On the death of General Taylor he succeeded to the Presidency and was inaugurated July 9, 1850. He formed a new Cabinet, all Whigs. It included Daniel Webster, Secretary of State, who was succeeded in 1852 by Edward Everett, of Massachusetts. Thomas Corwin of Ohio was his Secretary of the Treasury. For Secretary of War he first had General Scott, who was shortly followed by Charles M. Conrad, of Louisiana; John J. Crittenden, of Kentucky, was Attorney-General.

The year 1850 was prolific with disunion movements in the Southern States. The Senators who had joined with Calhoun in the address to the people, in 1849, united with their adherents in establishing at Washington a newspaper entitled "The Southern Press," devoted to the agitation of the slavery question; to presenting the advantages of disunion, and the organization of a Confederacy of Southern States to be called the "United States South." Its constant aim was to influence the South against the North, and advocated concert of action by the States of the former section. It was aided in its efforts by newspapers published in the South, more especially in South Carolina and Mississippi. The assembling of a Southern "Congress" was a turning point in the progress of disunion. Georgia refused to join; and her weight as a great Southern State was sufficient· to cause the failure of the scheme.

Although Congress had in 1790 and again in 1836 declared the policy of the Government to be non-

MILLARD FILLMORE.

interference with the States in respect to the matter of slavery within the limits of the respective States, the subject continued to be agitated. The subject first made its appearance in national politics in 1840, when James G. Birney was nominated by a party then formed favoring the abolition of slavery; it had a slight following which was largely increased at the election of 1844, when the same party again put the same ticket in the field, and received 62,140 votes. The efforts of the leaders of that faction were continued, and persisted in to such an extent, that when in 1848 it nominated a ticket, with Gerritt Smith for President, against the Democratic candidate, Martin Van Buren, the former received 296,232 votes. In the contest of 1852 the ticket had John P. Hale as its candidate for President, and polled 157,926 votes. This following was increased from time to time, until, uniting with a new party then formed, called the Republican party, which latter adopted a platform endorsing the views and sentiments of the abolitionists, the great and decisive battle for the principles involved was fought in the ensuing Presidential contest of 1856; when the candidate of the Republican party, John C. Fremont, supported by the entire abolition party, polled 1,341,812 votes.

On February 25, 1850, there were presented in the House of Representatives two petitions from citizens of Pennsylvania and Delaware, setting forth that slavery violates the Divine law; is inconsistent with Republican principles; that its existence has brought evil upon the country; and that no Union can exist with States which tolerate that institution; and asking that some plan be devised for the immediate, peaceful dissolution of the Union. The House re-

A SLAVE AUCTION IN THE SOUTH.

fused to receive and consider the petitions; as did also the Senate when the same petitions were presented the same month.

Slavery was abolished in the District of Columbia on September 17, 1850.

The election of 1852 was the last campaign in which the Whig party appeared in national politics. It nominated a ticket with Winfield Scott as its candidate for President. His opponent on the Democratic ticket was Franklin Pierce. A third ticket was placed in the field by the Abolition party, with John P. Hale as its candidate. The platform and declaration of principles of the Whig party were in substance an endorsement of the several measures embraced in Clay's compromise resolutions of the previous session of Congress, and the policy of a revenue for the economical administration of the Government, to be derived mainly from duties on imports, and by these means to afford protection to American industry. The main plank of the platform of the Abolition party (or Independent Democrats, as they were called) was for the non-extension and gradual extinction of slavery. The Democratic party equally adhered to the compromise measure. The election resulted in the choice of Franklin Pierce, by a popular vote of 1,601,474, and 254 electoral votes, against a popular aggregate vote of 1,542,403 (of which the abolitionists polled 157,926) and 42 electoral votes, for the Whig and abolition candidates. Pierce was duly inaugurated as President, March 4, 1853.

A new law for the reclamation of fugitive slaves was passed in 1850, containing substantially the same provisions as the law of 1793. The law authorizing the removal of the slave to the State from which he escaped, might be tolerated; but when all citizens were "commanded to aid in the execution of the law," its enforcement was practically nullified. The abolitionist and the humanitarian placed the moral law above the legal enactment, and acted accordingly. It was confidently expected that the President would refuse to give the bill his sanction. It met with his approval. Fillmore lost whatever chance he had of the nomination by his party, by signing and seeking to enforce the Fugitive Slave Law. He retired from office March 4, 1853, and returned to Buffalo. He was nominated in 1856 by the American party, but received no electoral votes but those of Maryland. He died March 8, 1874, and was buried in Buffalo, N. Y.

FRANKLIN PIERCE—1853-1857.

FRANKLIN PIERCE, our thirteenth President, was inaugurated March 4, 1853. He was born in New Hampshire, November 23, 1804. His father, General Benjamin Pierce, served throughout the Revolutionary War in his youth, and half a century later was twice elected Governor of New Hampshire. Franklin graduated at Bowdoin College in 1824, studied law, was soon a successful practitioner, and was elected to the State Legislature. He was sent to Congress in 1833, and re-elected for a second term, when he was advanced to the Senate, being its youngest member. He volunteered as a private in the Mexican War, where he rose to the rank of brigadier-general. He joined the army under Scott, by whom he was praised for his gallantry and discretion. At the close of the war he returned to Concord, resumed the practice of law, declining all political honors until the Democratic convention met in 1852. It was found that the four great competitors, Cass, Buchanan, Marcy, and Douglas, could not gain the requisite number of votes; so the Virginia delegation brought forward the name of General Pierce, and he was nominated by acclamation, carrying in the election all the States except four, against his illustrious rival, General Scott.

To his Cabinet he invited William L. Marcy as Secretary of State; James Guthrie of Kentucky was given the Treasury; Jefferson Davis of Mississippi was appointed War Secretary; and Caleb Cushing of Massachusetts was made Attorney-General.

On February 8, 1853, a bill passed the House of Representatives providing a territorial government for Nebraska, embracing all of what is now Kansas and Nebraska. It was silent on the subject of the repeal of the Missouri Compromise. The bill was tabled in the Senate, to be revived at the following session. It was amended to prohibit "alien suffrage." In the House this amendment was not agreed to, and the bill finally passed without it.

So far as Nebraska was concerned, no excitement of any kind marked the initiation of her territorial existence. Kansas was less fortunate. Her territory became at once the battle-field of a fierce political conflict between the advocates of slavery, and the free-soil men from the North who went there to resist the establishment of that institution in the

FRANKLIN PIERCE.

Territory. Differences arose between the Legislature and the Governor, brought about by antagonisms between the Pro-Slavery party and the **Free** State party; and the condition of affairs in Kansas assumed so frightful a mien in January, 1856, that the President sent a special Message to Congress on the subject; followed by a Proclamation, February 11, 1856, "warning all unlawful combinations (in the Territory) to retire peaceably to their respective abodes, or he would use the power of the local militia and the available forces of the U. S. to disperse them.

Applications were made for several successive years for the admission of Kansas as a State in the Union, upon the basis of three separate and distinct constitutions, all differing as to the main questions at issue between the contending factions. The name of Kansas was for some years synonymous with all that is lawless and anarchical. Elections became mere farces, and the officers thus fraudulently placed in power, used their authority only for their own or their party's interest. The party opposed to slavery at length triumphed; a constitution excluding slavery was adopted in 1859, and Kansas was admitted into the Union January 29, 1861.

The National party began preparations for a campaign in 1856. It aimed to introduce opposition to aliens and Roman Catholicism as a national question. On February 21, 1856, the National Council held a session at Philadelphia, and proceeded to formulate a declaration of principles. Among other things, it declared that ; Americans must rule America, and to this end, native-born citizens should be selected for all State, Federal, and municipal offices or Government employment, in preference to all others. No person shall be selected for political station who recognizes any allegiance or obligation, of any description, to any foreign prince, potentate, or power, or who refuses to recognize the Federal and State Constitutions as paramount to all other laws, as rules of political action. (This was a crack at the Pope.) A change in the laws of naturalization, making a continued residence of 21 years an indispensable requisite for citizenship hereafter, and excluding all paupers, and persons convicted of crime, from landing upon our shores, but no interference with the vested rights of foreigners. Opposition to any union between Church and State; no interference with religious faith, or worship, and no test oaths for office.

The convention was composed of 227 delegates, all the States being represented except Maine, Vermont, Georgia, and South Carolina. Millard Fillmore was nominated for President, and Andrew J. Donelson for Vice-President.

The Whig Convention endorsed the nominations made by the American party, and in its platform declared that "the Union is in peril, and our conviction is, that the restoration of Mr. Fillmore to the Presidency will furnish the best means of restoring peace."

The first National Convention of the new Republican party met at Philadelphia, June 18, 1856, and nominated John C. Fremont for President, and William L. Dayton for Vice-President. The Republican party, still composed of uncertain elements, sought only for a candidate that was available. Seward or Chase was the natural candidate. Both were fully identified with the principles and purposes of their party. Both were men of marked ability, strong in their respective States, each elected governor of his State and sure of its support; but Chase was opposed on account of his advanced opinions on the slavery question, and Seward was actively opposed by the so-called American party for his open hostility to its principles and policy. Thus it came to pass that public opinion gradually but strongly turned to John C. Fremont, who had no experience in public life, but who had attracted attention by his bold explorations in the West, and especially by his marching to California, and occupation of that Mexican territory.

This convention met in pursuance of a call addressed to the people of the United States, without regard to past political differences or divisions, who were opposed to the repeal of the Missouri Compromise; to the policy of President Pierce's Administration; to the extension of slavery into free territory, and in favor of the admission of Kansas as a free State, and of restoring the action of the Federal Government to the principles of Washington and Jefferson.

The Democrats of Pennsylvania nominated James Buchanan of Pennsylvania for President, and John C. Breckenridge of Kentucky for Vice-President; Pierce being his chief competitor, receiving 122 ballots on the first vote. Its platform declared (1) that the revenue to be raised should not exceed the actual necessary expenses of the Government, and for the gradual extinction of the public debt; (2) that the Constitution does not confer upon the general Government the power to commence and carry on a general system of internal improvements; (3) for a

JOHN C. FREMONT.
(*Major-General in the Union Army.*)

strict construction of the powers granted by the Constitution to the Federal Government; (4) that Congress has no power to charter a national bank; (5) that Congress has no power to interfere with slavery in the States and Territories; the people of which have the exclusive right and power to settle that question for themselves. (6) Opposition to native Americanism.

At the election which followed, the Democratic candidates were elected, though by a popular minority vote, having received 1,838,160 popular votes, and 174 electoral votes, against 2,215,768 popular votes, and 122 electoral votes for John C. Fremont, the Republican candidate, and Millard Fillmore, the Whig and American candidate.

Pierce's election was the last national contest in which the Whig party had an active share. It had never succeeded in breaking the power of its opponent. Twice its candidate had been elected, but in both cases success was due to the personal popularity and military reputation of the candidates. Both died early, one in a month, and the other in a trifle over a year after inauguration.

Franklin Pierce returned to private life, March 4, 1857. His administration was made entirely subservient to the interests of slavery. Whatever reputation it may have won was wholly due to Governor Marcy, whose wise management of our foreign affairs ranked him among the great men of our times. In 1863, Pierce made a speech at Concord against the Coercion of the Confederates. He died October 8, 1869, and was buried at Concord, New Hampshire.

JAMES BUCHANAN—1857-1861.

JAMES BUCHANAN, our fourteenth President, was born in Pennsylvania, April 23, 1791, and next to Harrison he was the oldest of the Presidents at the time of his election. He was well educated, studied law, and was admitted to practice in 1812. He was elected to his State Legislature when he was 23 years old. In 1822 he entered Congress, and continued till 1831, when he declined a re-election. Jackson sent him as Minister to Russia in 1832. On his return home in 1834 he was elected to the Senate, where he served till 1845, when he resigned his seat to become President Polk's Secretary of State. In 1853 Pierce appointed him Minister to England, where he remained till 1856. He was one of the three American Ministers who signed the document known as the "Ostend Manifesto," advising our Government to seize Cuba by force if it could not be purchased from Spain. With England, France, and Spain against us, seizing Cuba was, of course, out of the question. On his return he was nominated for the Presidency by the Democrats, and elected; was sworn into office March 4, 1857, and served out the full term of four years. In early life he was classed with the Federalists, but abandoned them on account of their opposition to the War of 1812. He ever afterwards acted with the Democrats.

Lewis Cass of Michigan was called to the State Department; Howell Cobb of Georgia was made Secretary of the Treasury; and John B. Floyd of Virginia was at the head of the War Department;

Jeremiah S. Black of Pennsylvania was appointed Attorney-General; Jacob Thompson of Mississippi was made Secretary of the Interior, and served out his full term; Isaac Toucey of Connecticut was Secretary of the Navy.

The advent of Mr. Buchanan was preceded by symptoms which looked like a general disruption of society, and he was hardly in a very hopeful mood when he delivered his inaugural. In that address, he stated that he had determined not to become a candidate for re-election, and would have no motive to influence his conduct, except the desire to serve his country, and to live in the grateful memory of his countrymen. They had recently, he observed, passed through a Presidential contest in which the passions of their fellow-citizens had been excited in the highest degree by questions of deep and vital importance. Referring to the Kansas difficulty, he said: "Congress is neither to legislate slavery into any Territory or State, nor to exclude it therefrom; but to leave the people thereof perfectly free to form and regulate their domestic institutions in their own way, subject only to the Constitution of the United States." Buchanan was not the man to condemn anything which favored the interests of the slave-holding States.

At the very outset of his Presidency the slave question was once more before the law courts. A negro, named Dred Scott, claimed his freedom on the score of residing in a State from which slavery had been excluded by the Missouri Compromise. In delivering judgment, the Supreme Court declared that the Missouri Compromise exceeded the powers of Congress by its invasion of State rights and sovereignty; that men of African race were not citizens

JAMES BUCHANAN.

of the United States; that the residence of a slave in a free State did not affect his legal condition on returning to a State where slavery was allowed by law; and that the negro had no rights which the white man was bound to respect. It was also decided that the ordinance of 1787, so far as it prohibited slavery from the North-west Territory, was unconstitutional. Thus all legislation against the extension of slavery, from the formation of the Constitution to that very year, was swept away at one blow. Such was the decision of the Democratic judges, who were in the majority; two other judges, who were Whigs, were in favor of the negro's claim. Great disappointment was felt at the North; but all such decisions helped forward the catastrophe by which slavery was blotted out forever.

A convention to frame a Constitution for Kansas met at Lecompton. A large majority of its members were in favor of establishing slavery in Kansas. All the white male inhabitants of the Territory above the age of 21 were entitled to vote. They were to vote by ballots which were endorsed, "Constitution with Slavery," and "Constitution with no Slavery." If the Constitution with no Slavery were carried, it was expressly declared that no slavery should exist in the State, excepting to this extent, that the right of property in slaves then in the Territory should not be interfered with. The exception was a serious one, because many slaveholders had gone there with their human cattle; but such was the tenderness of the convention towards these men that they were permitted to take advantage of their own wrong. To Buchanan, this arrangement seemed fair and admirable. Referring to the negroes already in the Territory, he said:—

The Free State settlers refused to vote, and the Lecompton Constitution *with* Slavery received 6000

A HOMESTEAD IN KANSAS.

majority. The President desired to admit Kansas under this Constitution. He was supported by all the Southern Congressmen; and opposed by the

Republicans and the "Douglas" Democrats. The Senate passed a bill for the admission of Kansas. It went to the House, where a proviso was tacked on to the bill sending it back to the people of Kansas for a new vote on the Lecompton Constitution, where it was rejected by more than 10,000 majority. A new Convention met at Wyandot in July, 1859, where a Constitution was adopted prohibiting slavery. This was submitted to the people and received a majority in its favor of over 4000 votes. So Kansas was admitted into the Union as a Free State, January 29, 1861.

The financial condition of the country, Buchanan described as without a parallel. The nation was positively embarassed by too large a surplus. Notwithstanding this, commercial panics created farspread ruin in the fall of 1857. A condition of general prosperity had existed for years, and it was declared that this had led to overtrading, and a serious revulsion set in. According to the President the troubles proceeded from a vicious system of paper-currency and bank credits exciting the people to wild speculations, and to gambling in stocks. In the midst of unsurpassed plenty in all the productions of agriculture and all the elements of national wealth, manufactures were suspended, public works retarded, private enterprises abandoned, and thousands of laborers thrown out of employment. There were about 1400 State Banks, acting independently of each other, and regulating their paper issues almost exclusively by a regard to the present interests of their stockholders.

CARRYING THE UNITED STATES MAIL ACROSS THE PRAIRIES, 1860.

171

No crisis was ever so unexpected, none ever culminated so rapidly, or proved so destructive. The commercial "suspensions" were wholly due to the breakdown of credit; the greater part were perfectly solvent, and able to resume as soon as the effects of the panic were over. It is important to observe that not only were the New York and Eastern banks perfectly solvent, but their notes were never mistrusted; and after the suspension of payments in specie, their notes continued to circulate at par. It was a run for *deposits* which shut up the banks; and a similar run would shut up every bank in existence. The crisis spread to England. The great London joint-stock banks and discount houses suspended, as did those in Hamburg, and the Bank of England, after increasing its discount rate from six to ten per cent. was forced to suspend specie payments. Then the tide turned.

A menacing question was the condition of Utah. Brigham Young was by Federal appointment the Governor of the Territory and Superintendent of Indian Affairs; he was at the same time head of the church called "the Latter-Day Saints," and professed to govern its members and dispose of their property by direct inspiration and authority from God. His power was therefore absolute over both Church and State; and if he chose that his government should come into collision with the General Government, the members of the Mormon Church would yield implicit obedience to his will. The position looked threatening, and it was made more difficult by the enormous distance the Federal troops had to traverse,

ON THE CENTRAL PACIFIC RAILROAD.

and the rugged and inhospitable desert which lay between them and their enemy. The trouble was temporarily quieted by a compromise; but the Mormon difficulty yet remained for more effectual settlement in later years. The Pacific Railroad was at that time only talked about.

In 1859 the Atlantic cable was successfully laid across the ocean, and America and Europe were united by telegraph. The first message occupied but thirty-five minutes in its transmission. The cable had been hastily manufactured, and was not fitted to bear the strain to which it was subjected. In a little while the insulation of the wire became faulty and the power of transmitting intelligence ceased. [So that through the War of the Rebellion, from 1861 to 1865, we could communicate with Europe only in the old-fashioned way.] A new company was formed in 1860. Various attempts were made, and, after repeated failures, the cable was finally laid in 1866; since which time it has been in successful operation between our shores and those of Great Britain.

The Pacific Railway was another great project of this time. Buchanan, in 1858, observed, "twelve months ago a road to the Pacific was held by many wise men to be a visionary subject. They had argued that the immense distance to be overcome, and the intervening mountains and deserts, were obstacles that could never be surmounted. We have seen mail-coaches with passengers, passing and repassing twice a week, by a common wagon-road, between San Francisco and St. Louis and Memphis, in less than twenty-five days;" and he urged that the Government should undertake the work as speedily as possible. Congress acknowledged the force of these words, and the Pacific Railway has been one of the greatest achievements of our genius, skill, and capital.

Before the end of Buchanan's Administration, and on the day that Sumter was fired upon by the Confederate Government, and while England and France and the rest of Europe were watching what they looked upon as the distinct "dissolution of the great American Union," and facetiously styling us the "Un*tied* States," the Representatives in Congress of "free men, free speech, free press, free soil, and freedom," were voting the expenditures necessary to build the Pacific Railway, uniting the Atlantic to to the Pacific Ocean, and proclaiming one undivided Nation!

John Brown, a native of Connecticut, had been for many years the terror of slave-holders. He was an Abolitionist. To him slavery was a sin, and to tolerate it in any way, or for any period, was a crime. He belonged to the farmer class, simple in manners, truthful in nature, fanatical in his convictions, and beyond the influence of fear. In Kansas he fought the Pro-Slavery party with courage, and often defeated them with loss. He had sons like himself, and two of these, who had settled in Kansas, were murdered by the "border ruffians."

He resolved to attack Harper's Ferry, in Virginia, and make it the starting-point of his attempt to rouse the negroes of the Southern States. He collected a band of 20 white men, and seized the Federal Armory at Harper's Ferry, where he was speedily joined by several hundred sympathizers. Arms were hastily despatched towards the South, and every inducement was held out to the negroes to engage in a general revolt.

Next morning the townspeople attacked the armory. Of course, Brown could not successfully repel any regular assault. He and his followers refused to surrender, but they were captured. Brown was wounded in several places in the final attack; his remaining two sons were slain; and others of his followers lay dead about the arsenal.

He had acted according to an imperative sense of duty; he had set his life upon a desperate cast, and, having failed, he was prepared to meet the consequences with that quiet courage which was a conspicuous part of his nature. He was 59 years old, rather small-sized, with keen, restless, gray eyes, and a grizzly beard and hair; wiry, active, and determined.

His conviction was a foregone conclusion, as the conviction of any man must be who is taken in the act of breaking the laws. He was warmly supported by the Northern Abolitionists; but more temperate politicians deplored the error he had committed, and saw there was no reasonable hope of his being spared. He was found guilty October 31, and was hung December 2, 1859. His companions were hung in March, 1860.

John Brown's attempt had failed. It was rash, hopeless, ill-advised, if we consider nothing but the immediate consequences; but it led to vast results in a future which was not distant. It made still more obvious the utter incompatibility of a Free

North and a Slave-holding South. It quickened throughout all the Northern States a passion of reforming zeal. It roused the fears and armed the hands of Southern planters, and made them comprehend that this dread question must be brought to an issue, fierce, agonizing, and conclusive. It caused both sides to understand their wishes and their will better than they had ever understood them before. It cleared away a mass of equivocations, evasions, compromises, and insincerities. It placed the moral law above the constitutional, and called sternly and sharply on all men to choose their color, and to abide by it. The coming Presidential election was determined beforehand by that Virginian execution: the victory of Abraham Lincoln dates from the defeat of Harper's Ferry.

JOHN BROWN.

The Democratic Convention met at Charleston, South Carolina, April 23, 1860. Caleb Cushing, from Massachusetts, presided.

Three years earlier, the man most favored by the Democrats, as their probable candidate at the next Presidential election, was Senator Douglas, of Illinois, whose Kansas-Nebraska Bill was held to have given him great claims on the South. But he considered that the slave-holders had gained enough, and he was unwilling to grant them anything more. He opposed Buchanan's zealous efforts to obtain the admission of Kansas to the Union as a slave State, and had thus earned the hatred of the extreme members of the Democratic party.

Before the balloting began, a reaffirmance of the two-thirds rule was resolved upon. It was well known that this resolution rendered the regular nomination of Douglas impossible.

The balloting began on the eighth day of the session. Necessary to a nomination, 202 votes. Douglas received 145½ votes; Mr. Hunter, of Virginia, 42; Mr. Guthrie, of Kentucky, 35½; with some few scattering votes.

There were 54 additional ballotings. Douglas never rose to more than 152½, and ended in 151½ votes.

In the hope that some compromise might be effected, the convention, adjourned to meet at Baltimore on June 18, 1860.

At this convention Douglas received 181½ votes, and was accordingly declared to be the regular nominee of the Democratic party of the Union.

Senator Fitzpatrick, of Alabama, was nominated

as the candidate for Vice-President, but declined the nomination, and it was conferred on Herschel

STEPHEN ARNOLD DOUGLAS.

V. Johnson, of Georgia, by the Executive Committee. Thus ended the Douglas Convention.

Another convention assembled at Baltimore on

June 23, styling itself the "National Democratic Convention." It was composed chiefly of the delegates who had withdrawn from the Douglas Convention, and the original delegates from Alabama and Louisiana. They abrogated the two-third rule, as had been done by the Douglas Convention. Both acted under the same necessity, because the preservation of this rule would have prevented a nomination by either.

Mr. Cushing presided here also.

The following names were presented to the convention for the nomination of President: John C. Breckenridge, of Kentucky, R. M. T. Hunter, of Virginia, Daniel S. Dickinson, of New York and Joseph Lane, of Oregon.

Eventually all these names were withdrawn except that of John C. Breckenridge, and he received the nomination by a unanimous vote. The whole number of votes cast in his favor from twenty States was 103½.

General Lane was nominated as the candidate for Vice-President. Thus terminated the Breckenridge Convention.

The Republicans met at Chicago, May 16, 1860. They were greatly encouraged by the large vote for Fremont and Dayton, and what had now become apparent as an irreconcilable division of the Democracy, encouraged them in the belief that they could elect their candidates. Those of the West were especially enthusiastic, and had contributed freely to the erection of an immense "Wigwam," capable of holding 10,000 people, at Chicago. All the Northern States were fully represented, and there were delegations from Delaware, Maryland, Kentucky, Missouri and Virginia, with occasional delegates from other Slave States, there being none, however, from the Gulf States. David Wilmot was chairman. No differences were excited by the report of the committee on platform, and the proceedings throughout were characterized by great harmony, though there was a sharp contest for the nomination. The prominent candidates were William H. Seward, of New York; Abraham Lincoln, of Illinois; Salmon P. Chase, of Ohio; Simon Cameron, of Pennsylvania, and Edward Bates, of Mis-

JOHN C. BRECKENRIDGE.

souri. There were three ballots, Lincoln receiving in the last 354 out of 446 votes. Seward led the vote at the beginning, but he was strongly opposed by gentlemen in his own State as prominent as Horace Greeley, the editor of the New York *Tribune*, the Republican organ of the country, and Thurlow Weed, the then political leader of New York State, and his nomination was thought to be inexpedient. Lincoln had been a candidate but a month or two before, while Seward's name had been everywhere canvassed, and where opposed in the Eastern and Middle States, it was mainly because of the belief that his views on slavery were too radical. He was more strongly favored by the Abolition branch of the party than any other candidate. When the news of his success was conveyed to Lincoln he read it in silence, and then announcing the result said: "There is a little woman down at our house would like to hear this—I'll go down and tell her," and he started amid the shouts of personal admirers. Hannibal Hamlin, of Maine, was nominated for Vice-President with much unanimity, and the Chicago Convention closed its work in a single day.

A "Constitutional Union," or an American Convention, met on May 9. Twenty States were represented, and John Bell of Tennessee, and Edward Everett of Massachusetts, were named for the Presidency and Vice-Presidency. Their friends, though known to be less in number than either those of Douglas, Lincoln or Breckenridge, yet made a vigorous canvass in the hope that the election would be thrown into the House, and that there a compromise

JEFFERSON DAVIS.
(President of the Southern Confederacy.)

in the vote by States would naturally turn toward their candidates. The result of this greatest contest is given below.

Lincoln received large majorities in nearly all of the free States, his popular vote being 1,866,452; electoral vote, 180. Douglas was next in the popular estimate, receiving 1,375,157 votes, with but 12 electors; Breckenridge had 847,953 votes, with 76 electors; Bell, with 570,631 votes, had 39 electors.

The principles involved in the controversy were briefly these: The Republican party asserted that slavery should not be extended to the Territories; that it could exist only by virtue of local and positive law; that freedom was national; that slavery was sectional and morally wrong, and the nation should at least anticipate its gradual extinction. The Douglas wing of the Democratic party adhered to the doctrine of popular sovereignty, and claimed that in its exercise in the Territories they were indifferent whether slavery was voted up or down. The Breckenridge wing of the Democratic party asserted both the moral and legal right to hold slaves, and to carry them to the Territories, and that no power save the national Constitution could prohibit or interfere with it outside of State lines. The Americans supporting Bell adhered to their peculiar doctrines touching emigration and naturalization, but had abandoned, in most of the States, the secrecy and oaths of the Know-Nothing order. They were evasive and non-committal on the slavery question.

The leaders in the South anticipated defeat at the election, and many of them made preparations for

A STREET IN NEW ORLEANS ON AN ELECTION DAY

the withdrawal of their States from the Union. Some of the more extreme anti-slavery men of the North, noting these preparations, for a time favored a plan of letting the South go in peace. South Carolina was the first to adopt a secession ordinance, and before it did so, Horace Greely said in the New York *Tribune:*

"If the Declaration of Independence justified the secession from the British Empire of three millions of colonists in 1776, we cannot see why it would not justify the secession of five millions of Southrons from the Federal Union in 1861."

These views fell into disfavor in the North, and the period of indecision on either side ceased when Fort Sumter was fired upon. The Gulf States openly made their preparations as soon as the result of the Presidential election was known.

South Carolina naturally led off in the secession movement. Her Senators and Representatives resigned from Congress early in November; her Ordinance of Secession was unanimously adopted on the 17th of November, 1860. The other Southern States quickly followed her example.

The Secession Ordinance passed in some of the States by the vote of their conventions, where they refused to submit the ordinance to a popular vote. In others, it was put to a general vote, manipulated by the leaders, and in all cases the vote was overwhelmingly in favor of the separation. In several States the governors ordered a repudiation by their citizens of all debts due to Northern men.

In Maryland, the governor declined to accept the

programme of Secession. Addresses for and against were frequent.

The Southern Congress met on February 4, 1861. Howell Cobb of Georgia was elected President and announced that secession "is now a fixed and irrevocable fact, and the separation is perfect, complete and perpetual." At this Congress were delegates from South Carolina, Georgia, Alabama, Louisiana, Florida and Mississippi. The Texas delegates were not appointed until February 14. A provisional Constitution was adopted, being the Constitution of the United States, with some changes. Jefferson Davis, of Mississippi, was chosen President, and Alexander H. Stephens, of Georgia, Vice-President. The laws and revenue officers of the United States were continued in the Confederate States until changed. Executive departments and a Confederate regular army were organized, and provision was made for borrowing money on March 11th, the permanent Constitution was adopted by Congress, and the first Confederate Congress was held, sitting from February 18, 1861, to April 21, 1862.

In the first Congress members chosen by rump State conventions, or by regiments in the Confederate service, sat for districts in Missouri and Kentucky, though these States had never seceded. There were thus thirteen States in all represented at the close of the first Congress; but as the area of the Confederacy narrowed before the advance of the Union armies, the vacancies in the second Congress became significantly more numerous. At its best the Confederate Senate numbered 26, and the House 106.

For four months between the Presidential election and the inauguration of Lincoln those favoring secession in the South had practical control of their section, for while Buchanan hesitated as to his Constitutional powers, the more active partisans in his Cabinet were aiding their Southern friends in every practical way.

The Confederate States was the name of the government formed in 1861 by the seven States which first seceded. Belligerent rights were accorded to it by the leading naval powers, but it was never recognized as a government, notwithstanding the persevering efforts of its agents at the principal courts. Lewis Cass resigned from the State Department, December 12, 1860, because the President declined to reinforce the forts in Charleston Harbor. Howell Cobb, the Treasury, "because his duty to Georgia required it."

John B. Floyd resigned as Secretary of War, because the President declined "to withdraw the garrison from the harbor of Charleston altogether." Before resigning he took care to transfer *all* the muskets and rifles from the Northern armories to arsenals in the South. All of these arms, except those sent to the North Carolina Arsenal, were seized by the States of South Carolina, Alabama, Louisiana and Georgia, and were no longer in possession of the United States.

Buchanan appealed to Congress to institute an amendment to the Constitution recognizing the rights of the Southern States in regard to slavery in the Territories:

THE CONFEDERACY INAUGURATED.

"I have purposely confined my remarks to revolutionary resistance, because it has been claimed within the last few years that any State, whenever this shall be its sovereign will and pleasure, may secede from the Union in accordance with the Constitution, and without any violation of the constitutional rights of the other members of the Confederacy. That as each became parties to the Union by the vote of its own people assembled in convention, so any one of them may retire from the Union in a similar manner by the vote of such a convention." * * * "I do not believe the Federal Government has the power to coerce a State."

Senator Crittenden brought forward a compromise proposition suggesting that amendments to the Constitution be made to "avert the danger of separation." Memorials from the North and from New England poured in favoring his views. The President exerted all his influence in favor of these peace measures. In his special Message to Congress, January 8, 1861, after depicting the consequences which had already resulted to the country from the bare apprehension of civil war and the dissolution of the Union, he said :

"Let the question be transferred from political assemblies to the ballot-box, and the people themselves would speedily redress the serious grievances which the South have suffered. But, in heaven's name, let the trial be made before we plunge into armed conflict upon the mere assumption that there is no other alternative."

This recommendation was totally disregarded. The

refusal to pass the Crittenden or any other compromise heightened the excitement in the South, where many showed great reluctance to dividing the Union. Georgia, though one of the cotton States, under the influence of conservative men like Alexander H. Stephens, showed greater concern for the Union than any other, and it took all the influence of spirits like that of Robert Toombs to bring her to favor secession. She was the most powerful of the cotton States and the richest, as she is to-day.

With the close of Buchanan's Administration all eyes turned to Lincoln, and fears were entertained that the date fixed by law for the counting of the electoral vote, February 15, 1861, would inaugurate violence and bloodshed at the seat of government. It passed peaceably. Both Houses met at noon in the House, Vice-President Breckenridge and Speaker Pennington, both Democrats, sitting side by side, and the count was made without challenge or question. A noted author of the time, thus epitomized the situation: "The Democratic Convention of 1856 nominated Buchanan for the Presidency as the champion of slavery; and his administration was conducted solely in the interests of that institution. If Buchanan had any generous sympathies for liberty, or aspirations for perpetuating the Republic, he gave no intimation of it in any of his public acts. He uttered no rebuke against the open declaration of secession, and his most trusted counsellors were the deepest plotters for the overthrow of the Union. Even while the fires of rebellion were being lighted, he plead impotency to quench them. And thus, with the mingled imputation of imbecility and treason, he retired from Washington, his retreating footsteps almost lit up by the torch of the incendiaries who were setting fire to the Capitol.

After his retirement from office he resided at Wheatland, Pennsylvania, where he died June 1, 1868.

ABRAHAM LINCOLN—1861-1865.

ABRAHAM LINCOLN, the sixteenth President, was born in Kentucky on February 12, 1809. Of his early years, he said himself in 1859: "My parents were both born in Virginia. My mother died in my tenth year. When I came of age I did not know much. I could read, write, and cipher to the rule of three, but that was all. The little advance I have now I picked up under the pressure of necessity. At 21, I came to Illinois. I was raised to farm-work, which I continued till I was 22 years old. When the Black Hawk War came on, in 1832, I was elected a captain of volunteers. In 1833 I was sent to the Legislature, and re-elected for three succeeding terms. During my legislative period I studied law, and removed to Springfield to practise it. In 1846 I was elected to the lower house of Congress. From 1849 to 1854 I practised law. I was always a Whig in politics."

In 1828 he made a trading voyage on a flatboat to New Orleans. Here the sight of slaves, chained and maltreated and flogged, was the origin of his deep convictions on the slavery question. In 1854 he had the great debate with Douglas. From this he gained great popularity. He was proposed for the

ABRAHAM LINCOLN'S EARLY HOME.

Senate in 1855, but after several ballots Lyman Trumbull was chosen.

When Fremont was nominated for the Presidency,

Lincoln was put forward for the Vice-Presidency, receiving 110 votes; but the place went to William L. Dayton. In 1858 he ran against Douglas for the Senate and was beaten. In 1860 the Republicans nominated him for the Presidency. He received the votes of every free State, while the votes of all the slave States were cast against him. He was unimpeachably elected, and on March 4, 1861, was inaugurated in Washington, surrounded by soldiers under command of General Scott; where he swore to "faithfully execute the office of President of the United States," and to the best of his ability, "preserve, protect, and defend the Constitution of the United States." In his address to Congress he said: "In *your* hands, my dissatisfied fellow-countrymen, and not in *mine*, is the momentous issue of civil war. The Government will not assail *you*. You can have no conflict without being yourselves the aggressors. *You* have an oath registered in heaven to destroy the Government, while I shall have the most solemn one to 'preserve, protect, and defend it.'"

To his Cabinet he called William H. Seward of New York as Secretary of State; Salmon P. Chase of Ohio to the Treasury; Simon Cameron of Pennsylvania to the War Office, and Edward Bates of Missouri was made Attorney-General. These gentlemen had been his rivals before the convention. The most eminent of these men was Seward. He was then about 60 years old, and had been connected with political affairs for 36 years. His principles were those of the Republican party, and he lost the nomination because it was feared his attitude in the slavery struggles would be too violent. When the "impending conflict" had come, he weakened before the threatened danger of separation, and considered

ABRAHAM LINCOLN.

that "the Constitution must be upheld at any cost." This lost him the support of **the Abolition element** in his party, who denounced him as a trimmer. He was a statesman of the world, and not disposed to risk his ends by rashness or scorn of compromise. His abilities and reputation marked him out for the chief post under the administration, and his name will always be closely associated with that of Lincoln. He expressed the view that "all troubles will be over in 90 days." Chase represented the more advanced anti-slavery element. Cameron, with a large business instinct, saw from the first that we were in for a prolonged war, in which the superior Northern resources and appliances would surely win.

On March 5, 1861, came the Commissioners appointed by the Confederate Government to open negotiations at Washington. Seward refused to recognize them on the ground that the States were acting illegally and in defiance of the Constitution. The Commissioners left on April 11, after addressing an angry communication repeating the assertions with regard to the right of secession, and denying the possibility of the Government ever winning back the seceding States, or subduing them by force.

Before Lincoln had entered office, most of the Southern forts, arsenals, docks, custom houses, etc., had been seized, and now that preparations were being made for active warfare by the Confederacy, many officers of the army and navy resigned or deserted, and joined it. The most notable was General Robert E. Lee, who for a time hesitated as to his "duty," but finally went with his State, Virginia. All officers were permitted to go, the administration not seeking to restrain any, under the belief that, until some open act of war was com-

WILLIAM H. SEWARD.

mitted, it ought to remain on the defensive. This was wise political policy, for it did more than all else to hold the Border States, the position of which Douglas understood fully as well as any statesman of that hour.

He was asked, "What will be the result of the efforts of Jefferson Davis, and his associates, to divide the Union?" "Rising, and looking, like one inspired, Douglas replied, 'The cotton States are making an effort to draw in the border States to their schemes of secession, and I am but too fearful they will succeed. If they do succeed, there will be the most terrible civil war the world has ever seen, lasting for years. Virginia will become a charnel house, but the end will be the triumph of the Union cause. One of their first efforts will be to take possession of this Capitol to give them prestige abroad, but they will never succeed in taking it—the North will rise *en masse* to defend it; but Washington will become a city of hospitals—the churches will be used for the sick and wounded.' The friend to whom this was said inquired, 'What justification for all this?' Douglas replied, 'There is NO justification, nor any pretence of any—if they remain in the Union, I will go as far as the Constitution will permit to maintain their just rights, and I do not doubt a majority of Congress would do the same. But if the Southern States attempt to secede from this Union, without further cause, I am in favor of their having just so many slaves, and just so much slave territory, as they can hold at the point of the bayonet, and NO MORE.'"

In the border States of Maryland, Virginia, North

Carolina, Tennessee and Missouri there were sharp political contests between the friends of secession and of the Union. Ultimately the Unionists triumphed in Maryland, Kentucky and Missouri—in

SALMON P. CHASE.

the latter State by the active aid of U. S. troops—in Maryland and Kentucky by military orders to arrest any members of the Legislature conspiring to take their States out. In Tennessee, the Union men, under the lead of Governor Andrew Johnson, made a gallant fight to keep the State in, and they had the sympathy of the majority of the people of East Tennessee. The leading Southerners encouraged the timid and hesitating by saying the North would not make war; that the political divisions would be too great there.

When the news flashed along the wires that Sumter had been fired upon, Lincoln immediately used his war powers and issued a call for 75,000 troops. All of the Northern Governors responded with promptness and enthusiasm.

The Southerners were more military than the Northerners; they were accustomed to the saddle and the use of firearms; the Northerners had to learn how to load and fire a gun after they joined the army. Several battles of little consequence were fought to secure control of Western Virginia. The Northern newspapers were clamoring for a forward movement. "On to Richmond," was the constant cry. On July 21, 1861, was fought the Battle of Bull Run. It was a severe one and the losses on both sides were heavy. The Confederates, being reinforced at the right moment, routed the Union Army, which fled back to Washington. It was now realized that we had entered into a war in earnest, and on July 22, 1861, Congress authorized the enlistment of 500,000 men, for a period not exceeding three years. Other large requisitions for volunteers were subsequently made. We shall not attempt to relate the history of the battles for the Union.

The last great battle was at Gettysburg, Pennsylvania, where General Lee was repulsed. He surrendered his army to General Grant on April 9, 1865. With the surrender of Lee, the last hope of Southern independence vanished.

During all the war period the Union newspapers published accounts of all the movements of the armies; the Confederates were constantly supplied with information by secession sympathizers; attempts

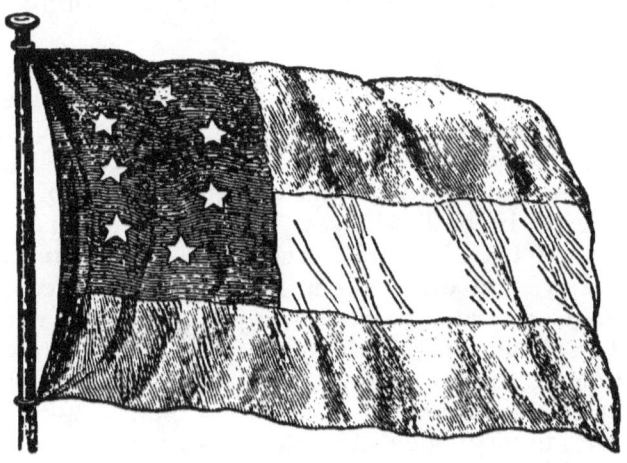

THE CONFEDERATE FLAG.

were made to release the Confederate prisoners of war; infected clothing was brought from Canada and sold in New York and elsewhere; attempts were made to burn the hotels in New York City. Opposition was made to the draft there and a riot ensued. The fury of the mob was several days beyond control, and troops had to be called from the front to suppress it. It was afterwards ascertained that Confederate agents really organized the riot as a movement to "take the enemy in the rear."

After this riot a more vigorous prosecution of the war was determined upon.

The Confederates conscripted all white men, residents of their States, between the ages of 17 and 50—as it was said, "everybody capable of bearing arms, from the cradle to the grave." Their newspapers were not allowed to make any mention of the military movements.

In March, 1862, Lincoln was impressed with the idea that great good would follow compensated emancipation in the Border States, and he suggested to Congress the passing of such a law. Various measures relating to compensated emancipation were considered in both Houses, but it was dropped in March, 1863. Lincoln determined upon a more radical policy, and on September 22, 1862, issued his celebrated proclamation declaring that he would emancipate "all persons held as slaves within any State or designated part of a State, the people whereof shall be in rebellion against the United States"—by the first of January, 1863, if such sections were not "in good faith represented in Congress." He followed this by actual emancipation at the time stated.

These proclamations were followed by many attempts on the part of the Democrats to declare them null and void; but all such were tabled. The House, on December 15, 1862, endorsed the first by a vote of 78 to 51, almost a strict party vote. Two classed as Democrats voted for emancipation; seven classed as Republicans voted against it.

On July 14, 1862, West Virginia was admitted into the Union. She had separated in the early years of the war from the mother State, which had seceded.

The capture of New Orleans led to the enrolment of 60,000 citizens of Louisiana as citizens of the United States. The President thereupon appointed a Military Governor for the entire State, and this Governor ordered an election for members of Congress under the old State Constitution. This was held December 3, 1862, when Flanders and Hahn were returned, neither receiving 3,000 votes. They received certificates, presented them, and thus opened up a new and grave political question. The Democrats opposed their admission. The vote stood 92 for to 44 against, almost a strict party test, the Democrats voting no.

On December 15, 1863, was passed the first Reconstruction Act, authorizing the President to appoint in each of the States declared in rebellion, a Provisional Governor; to be charged with the civil administration until a State government therein shall be recognized.

The Presidential election of 1864 came round. The Republicans renominated President Lincoln unanimously, save the vote of Missouri, which was cast for General Grant. Hannibal Hamlin was not renominated, because of a desire to give part of the ticket to the union men of the South, who pressed Andrew Johnson of Tennessee. There was some opposition to Lincoln's second nomination, which was dissipated by his homely remark that "it was bad policy to swap horses in crossing a stream." This emphasized the general belief.

The Democrats nominated General George B. McClellan of New Jersey for President, and George H. Pendleton of Ohio for Vice-President. General McClellan was made available for the Democratic nomination through certain political letters which

GENERAL GEORGE B. McCLELLAN.

he had written on points of difference between himself and the Lincoln Administration.

The Democratic platform carried this resolution, which sufficiently explains its attitude:

Resolved, That this convention does explicitly declare, as the sense of the American people, that after four years of failure to restore the Union by the experiment of war, during which, under the pretence of a military necessity of a war power higher than the Constitution, the Constitution itself has been disregarded in every part, and public liberty and private right alike trodden down, and the material prosperity of the country essentially impaired, justice, humanity, liberty, and the public welfare demand that immediate efforts be made for a cessation of hostilities, with a view to an ultimate convention of all the States, or other peaceable means, to the end that, at the earliest practicable moment, peace may be restored on the basis of the Federal Union of all the States.

Lincoln's views were well known; they were felt in the general conduct of the war. The campaign was exciting, and was watched by both armies with interest and anxiety. In this election, by virtue of an act of Congress, the soldiers in the field were permitted to vote, and a large majority of every branch of the service sustained the administration, though two years before, McClellan had been the idol of the Army of the Potomac. Lincoln and Johnson received 212 electoral votes, against 21 for McClellan and Pendleton.

In President Lincoln's second inaugural address, delivered on March 4, 1865, he spoke the following words, since oft quoted as typical of the kindly disposition of the man believed by his party to be the greatest President since Washington: "With malice toward none, with charity for all, with firmness in the right, as God gives us to see the right, let us strive on to finish the work we are in, to bind up the Nation's wounds, to care for him who shall have borne the battle, and for his widow and orphans—to do all which may achieve a just and lasting peace among ourselves and with all nations."

April, 1865, was a month of triumph and of mourning. In its earlier days, Richmond was occupied by the forces of the Union, and Lee surrendered to Grant. In its later days, Sherman achieved his final success, and the Confederacy, except in a few scattered members, lay dead before its foe. But between those two sets of events occurred a tragedy which had no parallel in American annals, which convulsed the nation with rage and grief. For the first time in the records of the Republic, political assassination struck down the head of the Government, and sought with hasty and murderous hands to settle the great problems of the day.

Lincoln had entered on his second term not more than six weeks when the bullet of an assassin closed his mortal career. He had nearly seen the end of the great contest for which his first election served as the pretext; but many difficulties yet remained to be overcome. The roughly-hewn, shaggy, uncouth face brightened now and then with its pleasant and genial smile; but the lines were more deeply furrowed than they had been a few years before, and the shadows of vast responsibilities gave something of sublimity to features that were homely in themselves.

Lincoln visited Ford's theatre in Washington where he was shot in the head by an actor named

Wilkes Booth. Booth fled to virginia, where he was hunted down by a party of cavalry and shot.

Lincoln lingered for several hours, but on the morning of April 15th, he breathed his last. About the same time that the murder of the President was being committed, an attempt was made to assassinate Secretary Seward.

In the agitation of the public mind consequent on these daring and extraordinary crimes, it was not unreasonably believed that a vast conspiracy had been planned by Southern politicians, to effect by murder what they could not accomplish by military force.

The funeral of Abraham Lincoln was conducted with unexampled solemnity and magnificence. The coffin was carried on a huge catafalque, where it could be viewed by the multitudes in the various cities through which the funeral cortege passed, on its way from Washington to Oak Ridge Cemetery, near Springfield, Illinois, where he was buried May 4, 1865. His remains were placed in an appropriate tomb on October 15, 1874.

ANDREW JOHNSON—1865-1869.

ANDREW JOHNSON, our seventeenth President, was inaugurated on the same morning that Lincoln died. No man thus called to administer a great Government could have satisfied his party; and he went through his term with little peace or success.

He was born in North Carolina, December 29, 1808. He was born in the obscurest poverty, and received no schooling. At ten he was apprenticed to a tailor. While a young man, he started for Tennessee with his widowed mother to find a home. Ambitious to better his condition, he became his own teacher. Marrying a girl of superior intelligence, she taught him to write and cipher. He dashed into local politics; he rose steadily, step by step, to the State Senate; then to Congress, where he remained ten years. He was twice elected Governor of Tennessee, and in 1857 was sent to the Senate. Thus his acquaintance with political life was not small, or wanting in variety. Like most self-made men, he was a little ostentatious in talking about his plebeian origin, and of what he owed to the people. But his conduct in the Senate showed him to be a man of sense and moderation. He carried through the Homestead Law, for which his name is gratefully remembered in many homes throughout the broad West. At the beginning of the war Lincoln appointed him the Military Governor of Tennessee, where he distinguished himself by vigor and resolution, and nerved the hunted friends of the Union.

At the start of his Presidential career he seemed to range himself on the side of the most extreme Northern politicians, and against those who were in favor of adopting a more conciliatory policy towards the South—an impression which his subsequent conduct entirely removed. He said the time had arrived when the American people should understand that treason was a crime. To the mass of the misled he would say, "Mercy, clemency, reconciliation, and the restoration of local government;" but to the

ANDREW JOHNSON.

conscious, influential traitor, who had attempted to destroy the life of the nation, he would say: "On you be inflicted the severest penalty of your crime. Mercy without justice would in itself be criminal."

From evidence in the Bureau of Military Justice, he thought the assassination of Abraham Lincoln and the attempted assassination of Wm. H. Seward, had been procured by Jefferson Davis, Clement C. Clay, Jacob Thompson, and "other rebels and traitors harbored in Canada." The evidence, however, showed that the scheme was harebrained, and from no responsible political source. The proclamation, however, gave keenness to the search for the fugitive Davis, and he was captured while making his way through Georgia to the Florida coast, with the intention of escaping from the country. He was imprisoned in Fortress Monroe, and an indictment for treason was found against him; but he remained a close prisoner for nearly two years, until times when political policies had been changed or modified. Horace Greeley was one of his bondsmen. By this time there was grave doubt whether he could be legally convicted, now that the charge of inciting Booth's crime had been tacitly abandoned. Webster (in his Bunker Hill oration) had only given clearer expression to the American doctrine, that, after a revolt has levied a regular army, and fought therewith a pitched battle, its champions, even though utterly defeated, cannot be tried and convicted as traitors. This may be an extreme statement; but a rebellion which has for years maintained great armies, levied taxes and conscriptions, negotiated loans, fought scores of sanguinary battles with alternate successes and reverses, and exchanged tens of thousands of prisoners of war, can hardly fail to have achieved thereby the position and the rights of a lawful belligerent.

This view, as then presented by Greeley, was accepted by the President, who from intemperate denunciation had become the friend of his old friends in the South. Greeley's view was not generally accepted by the North, though most of the leading men of both parties hoped the responsibility of a trial would be avoided by the escape and flight of the prisoner. But he was confident by this time, and sought a trial. He was never tried, and the best reason for the fact is that no conviction was possible, except by packing a jury.

On April 29, 1865, Johnson issued a proclamation removing all restrictions upon internal, domestic and coastwise and commercial intercourse in all Southern States east of the Mississippi; the blockade was removed May 22, and on May 29 a proclamation of amnesty was issued, with fourteen classes excepted therefrom, and the requirement of an "ironclad oath" from those accepting its provisions. Proclamations rapidly followed in shaping the lately rebellious States to the conditions of peace and restoration to the Union. These States were required to hold conventions, repeal secession ordinances, accept the abolition of slavery, repudiate Southern war debts, provide for Congressional representation, and elect new State officers and legislatures. The several Constitutional amendments were, of course, to be ratified by a vote of the people. These conditions were eventually all complied with, some of the States being more tardy than others.

It is not partisanship to say that Johnson's views underwent a change. So radical had this difference become that he vetoed nearly all of the political bills passed by the Republicans from 1866 until the end of his administration, but such was the Republican preponderance in both Houses of Congress that they passed them over his head by the necessary two-thirds vote. He vetoed the several Freedmen's Bureau Bills, the Civil Rights Bill, that for the admission of Nebraska and Colorado, the Bill to permit Colored Suffrage in the District of Columbia, one of the Reconstruction Bills, and finally made a direct issue with the powers of Congress by his veto of the Civil Tenure Bill.

General Butler charged the President with "attempting to bring Congress into disgrace, ridicule, hatred, contempt, and reproach, and with delivering intemperate, inflammatory, and scandalous harangues, accompanied by threats and bitter menaces against Congress and the laws of the United States." Assuredly nothing could be more reprehensible than the language employed by the President on many public occasions in characterizing Congress as a "rump" and charging in substance that they were not a Congress authorized to execute legislative power, but on the contrary, represented only part of the States. It was therefore resolved to impeach him.

The impeachment trial began on March 30, 1866. There being 27 States represented, there were 54 Senators, who constituted the court, presided over by Chief Justice Chase. Many of the speeches for and against the impeachment were distinguished by great brilliancy and power. The vote resulted in 35 for conviction and 19 for acquittal. The Constitution requiring a vote of two-thirds to convict, the President was therefore acquitted. And so the trial ended.

The political differences between the President and the Republicans were not softened by the attempted impeachment, and singularly enough the failure of their effort did not weaken the Republicans as a party. They were so well united that those who disagreed with them passed, at least temporarily, from public life, some of the ablest, like Senators Trumbull and Fessenden, retiring permanently. The President pursued his policy, save where he was hedged by Congress, until the end, and retired to his native State after Grant was inaugurated on March 4, 1869. He tried to get back to the Senate in 1870, but was defeated; he was, however, elected in 1875, and took his seat in the extra session in March. Great expectations were built upon his return to the Senate, but he died ere the anticipations could be fulfilled, on July 31, 1875. He was buried at Greenville, Tennessee.

In 1867, Secretary Seward obtained an important addition to our territory by the purchase of Russian America, in the extreme north-west of the continent, for $7,000,000. This is called Alaska; and is on the other side of Canada. Some dissatisfaction was found with the purchase, as being of little commercial value, with Canada separating the two sections; but Canada, by the irresistible force of events, is destined at no very distant day to voluntarily annex herself to the United States, to participate in the enormous advantage sure to accrue to her by such union. Then the entire northern continent is ours.

While our war was progressing, Napoleon III of France, conceived the idea of establishing an empire in Mexico. An Austrian archduke, Maximilian, had been enthroned with French soldiers to support his occupation. This was an invasion of our "Monroe Doctrine" principle; but we could take but little notice of what was going on outside our own Union. At the end of 1865 a protest was made. Napoleon withdrew his troops during 1866. Juarez, the President of the Republic of Mexico, compelled Maximilian to surrender, May 15, 1867; he was condemned by a council of war, and shot on June 19, 1867; and this ended the short-

SEYMOUR AND BLAIR.

lived Mexican Empire. The fact that Napoleon withdrew his troops at the bidding of President Johnson, and that the empire thereupon tumbled into ruins, was certainly a great triumph of American policy.

The Republican Convention nominated with unanimity, General Ulysses S. Grant, of Illinois, for President, and Schuyler Colfax, of Indiana, for Vice-President. The Democratic Convention met in New York City, July 4. Governor Horatio Seymour, of New York, was nominated for President on the 22d ballot, and Francis P. Blair, Jr., of Missouri, for Vice-President.

Grant carried all of the States save eight, receiving an electoral vote of 214 against 80.

ULYSSES S. GRANT—1869–1877.

ULYSSES SIMPSON GRANT, the eighteenth President, was descended from Scotch ancestors, and born in Ohio, December 27, 1822, and was the youngest elected President. His parents were natives of Pennsylvania. Having acquired the rudiments of education at a common school, and having a taste for military life, he was sent to West Point in 1839. He was a diligent student, but not bright and graduated in 1843, standing twenty-first in a class of thirty-nine. He was made a brevet-lieutenant of infantry, and attached to the Fourth Regiment, his regiment being ordered to Texas, to join the army of General Taylor. Our young lieutenant fought his first battle at Palo Alto. He was also in the battles at Resaca, Monterey, and at the siege of Vera Cruz. At Molina del Rey, he was appointed on the field a first lieutenant for his gallantry; and for his conduct at Chapultepec he was breveted a captain. In 1854 he resigned, and attempted various kinds of business without success. In 1848 he married. On the first call for troops to suppress the Rebellion, he marched in command of a company of volunteers to Springfield. He was appointed a colonel in June, and became a brigadier-general in August, 1861. He rose to Lieutenant-General in March, 1864, when he had command of all the armies of the Republic, which then numbered nearly 750,000 men. In this new position his unrivalled generalship was fully displayed. Having brought the war to an end, he was promoted to the rank of General—specially created —and took his proper station by the side of the great "Captains of the World." He was triumphantly elected to the Presidency in 1868; inaugurated March 4, 1869; and re-elected four years later.

His first battle in the Rebellion was fought at Belmont, Missouri, on November 7, 1861. Both sides claimed the victory. In February, 1862, he took Fort Henry, and a week later Fort Donelson, which was garrisoned with 20,000 men. It was here that he used his celebrated sentence, "No terms other than unconditional, immediate surrender can be accepted. I propose to move immediately upon your works." The fort surrendered, and Grant was at once made a Major-General. He was now styled "Unconditional Surrender Grant." On July 4, 1863, Vicksburg was captured, causing great exultation among the friends of the Union. He was rewarded for this service by promotion to the rank of Major-General in the *Regular* Army. Captain

ULYSSES S. GRANT.

Porter and the gunboats co-operated in this capture. Up to this time Grant had taken 90,000 prisoners;

while disaster seemed to follow all the commanders operating against Richmond. On March 12, 1864, he was appointed commander of all the armies. He himself directed the army in Virginia, battling with Robert E. Lee; and sent William T. Sherman to oppose the other Confederate army operating in Georgia, and commanded by Joseph E. Johnston. Philip H. Sheridan commanded all of the cavalry in Grant's Army of the Potomac. Lee and Johnston were trained West Point soldiers; able, alert, and indefatigable. On May 5, 1864, Grant's army met the enemy in the great but indecisive battle of the Wilderness. On June 3, he attacked the enemy's works at Cold Harbor, but was repulsed with heavy loss. He remained nearly inactive before Petersburg during the winter of 1864–1865; but Sherman continued moving up from Georgia to Virginia. It had now got to be, as was expressed by the Democratic press, "a mere question of bloody arithmetic." Lee was surrounded; his army were starving; it was criminal to pursue the contest any longer. Richmond was evacuated April 2, and on the ninth of April, 1865, Lee surrendered at Appomattox Court House, Virginia; after which the insurgents everywhere gave up the contest. On his election to the Presidency he resigned his supreme rank to General Sherman.

The war debt at the end of 1865 was three billions of dollars—to say nothing of the frightful loss of life. Such was the enormous cost which the slaveholders' rebellion imposed upon the land; but the end has been attained, and the people had sufficient confidence in the elasticity of our resources to bear with cheerfulness this burden, which a few years had accumulated, on their shoulders.

Grant was inaugurated, and the Congressional plan of reconstruction was rapidly pushed, with at first very little opposition save that manifested by the Democrats in Congress. The conditions of re-admission were the ratification of the thirteenth and fourteenth constitutional amendments.

On February 25, 1869, the fifteenth amendment was added to the list by its adoption in Congress and submission to the States. It conferred the right of suffrage on all citizens, without distinction of "race, color or previous condition of servitude." By March 30, 1870, it was ratified by twenty-nine States, the required three-fourths of all in the Union. The issue was shrewdly handled, and in most instances met Legislatures ready to receive it. Many of the Southern States were specially interested in its passage, since a denial of suffrage would abridge their representation in Congress. This was, of course, true of all the States; but its force was indisputable in sections containing large colored populations.

The 41st Congress met December 4, 1869, and before its close Virginia, Georgia, Texas and Mississippi had all complied with the conditions of reconstruction, and were re-admitted to the Union. This practically completed the work of reconstruction.

Congress met December 5, 1870. Grant's Message discussed a new question, and advocated the annexation of San Domingo to the United States. A treaty had been negotiated between President Grant and the President of the Republic of San

Domingo, September 4, 1869, but it was rejected by the Senate. The question had no political significance. No territory could be annexed without a treaty, and this must be ratified by two-thirds of the Senate; and as this could not be commanded, the project was dropped. It has not since attracted any attention.

The long-disputed Alabama Claims of the United States against Great Britain, arising from the depredations of the Anglo-rebel privateers, built and fitted out and manned in British waters, were referred by the Treaty of Washington, dated May 8, 1871, to arbitrators, and this was the first and most signal triumph of the plan of arbitration, so far as the United States was concerned. The arbitrators were appointed, at the invitation of the Governments of Great Britain and the United States, from these powers, and from Brazil, Italy, and Switzerland. On September 14, 1872, they gave to the United States gross damages to the amount of $15,500,000.

The Civil Service Reform Bill was passed at this session. When first proposed, partisan politics had no part or place in civil service reform, and the author of the plan was himself a distinguished Republican. In fact, both parties thought something good had been reached, and there was practically no resistance at first to a trial.

Efforts were made to pass bills to remove the political disabilities of former Southern rebels. All such efforts were defeated by the Republicans. The Amnesty Bill, however, was passed May 22, 1872, after an agreement to exclude from its provisions all who held the higher military and civic positions under the Confederacy—in all about 350 persons. Subsequently acts removing the disabilities of all save Jefferson Davis were passed.

An issue raised in Missouri gave rise to the *Liberal Republican party*. In 1870 the Republican party, then in control of the Legislature of Missouri, split into two parts on the question of the removal of the disqualifications imposed upon rebels by the State Constitution during the war. Those favoring the removal of disabilities were headed by B. Gratz Brown and Carl Schurz, and they called themselves Liberal Republicans; those opposed were called and accepted the name of Radical Republicans. The former quickly allied themselves with the Democrats, and thus carried the State, though Grant's administration backed the Radicals with all the power of the Government. As a result the disabilities were removed, and the Liberals sought to promote a reaction in Republican sentiment all over the country. Greeley was the recognized head of this movement, and he was ably aided by leading Republicans in nearly all of the States, who at once began to lay plans to carry the next Presidential election.

They charged that the Enforcement Acts of Congress were designed more for the political advancement of Grant's adherents than for the benefit of the country; that instead of suppressing they were calculated to promote a war of races in the South; that Grant was seeking the establishment of a military despotism, etc. These leaders were all brilliant men.

In the spring of 1871 the Liberal Republicans and Democrats of Ohio prepared for a fusion, and after frequent consultations of the various leaders with Mr. Greeley, a call was issued from Missouri on January 24, 1872, for a Convention of the Liberal

HORACE GREELEY.

Republican party to be held at Cincinnati, May 1. The well-matured plans of the leaders were carried out in the nomination of Horace Greeley, of New

York, the editor of the New York *Tribune*, for President, and B. Gratz Brown, of Missouri, for Vice-President, though not without a serious struggle over the chief nomination, which was warmly contested by the friends of Charles Francis Adams.

The original leaders now prepared to capture the Democratic Convention. By nearly a unanimous vote it was induced to endorse the Cincinnati platform, and it likewise finally endorsed Greeley and Brown—though not without many bitter protests. A few straight-out Democrats met later and nominated Charles O'Conor, of New York, for President, and John Quincy Adams, of Massachusetts, for Vice-President, and these were kept in the race to the end, receiving a popular vote of about 30,000.

The regular Republican Convention renominated President Grant unanimously, and Henry Wilson, of Massachusetts, for Vice-President. This change to Wilson was to favor the solid Republican States of New England, and to prevent both candidates coming from the West.

Grant and Wilson received nearly 3,600,000 popular votes, while Greeley and Brown polled 2,835,000 votes. Grant and Wilson receiving 286 electoral votes to 47 only for Greeley and Brown, they were declared elected and duly inaugurated, March 4, 1873. Horace Greeley died soon afterwards in an insane asylum. The *Tribune*, the national organ of the Republicans for 30 years, lost caste, and this, and the defeat for the Presidency, unbalanced poor Greeley's mind.

By 1874 the Democrats of the South, who then generally classed themselves as Conservatives, had gained control of all the State Governments except those of Louisiana, Florida and South Carolina. In nearly all, the Republican Governments had called upon President Grant for military aid in maintaining their positions, but this was declined except in the

CHARLES O'CONOR.

presence of such outbreaks as the proper State authorities could not suppress. In Arkansas, Alabama, Mississippi, and Texas, Grant declined to interfere. The cry came from the Democratic partisans in the South for home-rule; another came from the negroes that they were constantly disfranchised, intimidated and assaulted by the White League, a body of men organized in the Gulf States for the purpose of breaking up the "carpet-bag government."

PETER COOPER.

On July 1, 1876, the Centennial of the Declaration of Independence was greeted with rejoicing in every town and city in the land. On May 10, the Centennial Exposition, in Philadelphia, was opened by General Grant. For six years preparations had been making to have an exhibition designed to show the nation's progress during its first century of existence. All the world was invited to contribute examples of their products and industries. It was the largest display of the kind made up to that time, the covered space being over 60 acres, and the cost of the buildings was over $6,000,000. It was open for six months; and great crowds gathered from all over the world to examine the myriads of objects exhibited. There were 30,000 exhibitors; 33 foreign countries were represented; over 10,000,000 visitors gathered there; and the admission receipts ran up to $4,000,000.

Colorado was admitted as the 38th State on August 1, 1776.

Our original 13 States, with their population of 4,000,000, had grown to 38 States with nearly 60,000,000 people, and wealth, comfort and education and art flourished in still larger proportion.

The people had grown tired of Credit Mobilier, Whiskey Ring, Indian Tradership, Salary Grab, and other scandals; and some sort of a change was imperatively demanded. As a consequence the 44th Congress, which met in December, 1875, had been changed by what was called "the tidal wave," from Republican to Democratic, and Michael C. Kerr, of Indiana, was elected Speaker. The Senate remained Republican, but with a reduced margin.

The troubles in the South, and the almost general overthrow of the "carpet-bag government," impressed all with the fact that the Presidential election of 1876 would be exceedingly close and exciting, and the result confirmed this belief. The

Greenbackers were the first to meet and Peter Cooper, of New York, was nominated for President, and Samuel F. Cary, of Ohio, for Vice-President.

The Republicans met, with James G. Blaine recognized as the leading candidate. Grant had been named for a third term, and there was a belief that his name would be presented. Such was the feeling on this question that the Houses of Congress and a Republican State Convention in Pennsylvania had passed resolutions declaring that a third term for President would be a violation of the "unwritten law" handed down through the examples from Washington to Jackson. His name, however, was not then presented. The "unit rule" at this convention was for the first time resisted, and by the friends of Blaine, with a view to release from instructions of State Conventions some of his friends. New York had instructed for Conkling and Pennsylvania for Hartranft. The chairman decided against the binding force of the unit rule, and to assert the liberty of each delegate to vote as he pleased. The Convention sustained the decision on an appeal.

The balloting is here appended.

	1st Ballot.	2d.	3d.	4th.	5th.	6th.	7th.
Blaine	285	296	292	293	287	308	351
Conkling	113	114	121	126	114	111	21
Bristow	99	93	90	84	82	81	
Morton	124	120	113	108	95	85	
Hartranft	58	63	68	71	69	50	
Hayes	61	64	67	68	102	113	384

Rutherford B. Hayes, of Ohio, was nominated for President, and Wm. A. Wheeler, of New York, for Vice-President.

The Democrats met at St. Louis. Both the unit and the two-thirds rule were observed in this body. On the second ballot, Samuel J. Tilden, of New York, had 535 votes to 203 for all others. His leading competitor was Thomas A. Hendricks, of Indiana, who was nominated for Vice-President.

In the election that followed, Hayes and Wheeler carried all the Northern States except Connecticut, New York, New Jersey and Indiana; Tilden and Hendricks carried all of the Southern States except South Carolina, Florida and Louisiana. The three last-named States were claimed by the Democrats, but the members of the Congressional Investigating Committee quieted rival claims as to South Carolina by agreeing that it had fairly chosen the Republican electors. So close was the result that success or failure hinged upon the returns of Florida and Louisiana, and for days and weeks conflicting stories and claims came from these States. The Democrats claimed that they had won on the face of the returns from Louisiana, and that there was no authority to go behind these.

Congress met December 5, 1876, and while by that time all knew the dangers of the approaching electoral count, yet neither House would consent to the revision of the joint rule regulating the count. The Republicans claimed that the President of the Senate had the sole authority to open and announce the returns in the presence of the two Houses; the Democrats plainly disputed this right, and claimed that the joint body could control the count under the law.

There was grave danger, and it was asserted that the Democrats, fearing the President of the Senate would exercise the power of declaring the result, were preparing first to forcibly and at last with secrecy swear in and inaugurate Tilden.

President Grant and Secretary of War Cameron thought the condition of affairs critical, and both made active though secret preparations to secure the safe if not the peaceful inauguration of Hayes. Grant, in one of his sententious utterances, said he "would have peace if he had to fight for it." Members of Congress representing both of the great political parties substantially agreed upon an Electoral Commission Act. The leaders on the part of the Republicans in these conferences were Conkling, Ed-

SAMUEL J. TILDEN.

munds, Frelinghuysen; on the part of the Democrats, Bayard, Gordon, Randall and Hewitt, the latter a member of the House and Chairman of the Democratic Committee.

The Electoral Commission, composed of 8 Republicans and 7 Democrats, met February 1, 1877, and by uniform votes of 8 to 7 decided all objections to the electoral vote of Florida, Louisiana, South Carolina, and Oregon, in favor of the Republicans; and while the two Houses disagreed on nearly all of these points by strict party votes, the electoral votes were, under the provisions of the law, given to Hayes and Wheeler, and the final result declared to be 185 electors for Hayes and Wheeler, to 184 for Tilden and Hendricks. The uniform vote of 8 to 7 on all important propositions considered by the Electoral Commission, to their minds showed a partisan spirit, the existence of which it was difficult to deny. The action of the Republican "visiting statesmen" in Louisiana, in practically overthrowing the Packard or Republican government there, caused distrust and dissatisfaction in the minds of the more radical Republicans, who contended with every show of reason that if Hayes carried Louisiana, Packard, the Republican nominee for governor, must also have done so. The only sensible excuse for seating Hayes on the one side and throwing out Governor Packard on the other, was a desire for peace in the settlement of both Presidential and Southern State issues. There was hardly any question but that Tilden was elected; but he lacked the nerve and force of character to assert his rights. He "dreaded civil war." In the formation of the Electoral Commission, the

Democrats were out-generaled and everywhere out-manœuvered by their keener opponents. The banking and commercial class did not want any change of administration that might change the existing order of things, financially or industrially, and so there was an indifferent sort of acquiescence in the accepted political arrangements.

The question of the title of President was finally settled June 14, 1878, by the House Judiciary Committee, under the following resolution:

Resolved, That the two Houses of the 44th Congress having counted the votes cast for President and Vice-President of the United States, and having declared Rutherford B. Hayes to be elected President, and William A. Wheeler to be elected Vice-President, there is no power in any subsequent Congress to reverse that declaration, nor can any such power be exercised by the courts of the United States, or any other tribunal that Congress can create under the Constitution.

After retiring from his eight years' Presidency, Grant went on a voyage around the world. He was everywhere received with marked cordiality and treated as a potentate. The military governments of Europe flocked to see the victorious general who had put down the great rebellion. The junketing round the world kept him favorably before the public, and kept him out of the way of any political entanglements until the time should come round again for the nomination of Presidential candidates in 1880, when it was the avowed intention of his friends to spring his name again on the convention. This was popularity called a "third term," though not a third consecutive term. His three powerful senatorial friends, in the face of bitter protests, had secured the instructions of their respective State conventions for Grant. Conkling had done this in New York, Cameron in Pennsylvania, Logan in Illinois; but in each of the three States the opposition was so impressive that no serious attempts were made to substitute other delegates for those which had previously been selected by their Congressional districts. As a result there was a large minority in the delegations of the States opposed to the nomination of Grant, solely on the "third term" issue, and their votes could only be controlled by the enforcement of the unit rule. Senator Hoar, of Massachusetts, the President of the Convention (as did his predecessors in the Hayes Convention), decided against its enforcement, and as a result all the delegates were free to vote upon either State or district instructions, or as they chose. The convention was in session three days.

Grant, to his credit be it said, wrote a letter to Cameron refusing to allow his name to come before the convention for a third term. This letter was ruthlessly suppressed by Conkling. The fact that such a letter had been written was not made public till the fall of 1895; and the good name of Grant suffered greatly in consequence.

Grant started in the ballotings with 304 votes, which rose to 306, where it stayed for 36 ballots; 378 votes were necessary for a choice. Blaine received 284, and they stuck to him with the same persistency throughout. Sherman and Blaine, to defeat Grant, threw their delegations to James A. Garfield who received 399 votes on the 36th ballot, and was declared the nominee. [For particulars of the balloting, see under Hayes.]

Grant engaged with his son in the banking business in New York City, under the name of Grant & Ward. The business turned out disastrously. In 1885, after his bankruptcy, he undertook the compilation of his "Memoirs," and completed the work only four days before his death. The sale of the book was something unprecedented, and brought to his widow in royalties over half a million dollars.

His last home was in New York. He fell sick in 1884, and after a painful eight months' lingering, with cancer in the throat, he died at Mount McGregor, near Saratoga, July 23, 1885, and was buried with great pomp, August 8, 1885, at Riverside Park (on the Hudson), New York City.

RUTHERFORD B. HAYES—1877-1881.

RUTHERFORD BIRCHARD HAYES, the nineteenth President, was born in Ohio, Oct. 4, 1822. He graduated in Kenyon College, Ohio, in 1842, and having studied law at Harvard College, in Massachusetts, moved to Cincinnati, where he practised from 1849 to 1861. He served with distinction in the Civil War as an officer of volunteers, being once severely wounded, and he rose to the rank of brevet-major-general. He was sent to Congress in 1865; was elected Governor in 1867, being re-elected in 1869, and again in 1875. In 1876 he was nominated by the Republicans for the Presidency; was declared elected by the Electoral Commission, and was inaugurated March 4, 1877.

William M. Evarts of New York, the ablest man in the State, was appointed Secretary of State; and John Sherman of Ohio, was given the Treasury Department.

From the very beginning the administration of Hayes had not the cordial support of the party, nor was it solidly opposed by the Democrats, as was the last administration of Grant. His early withdrawal of the troops from the Southern States—and it was this withdrawal and the suggestion of it from the "visiting statesmen" which overthrew the Packard government in Louisiana—embittered the hostility of many radical Republicans. Senator Conkling, who always disliked the President, was conspicuous in his opposition, as was Logan of Illinois, and Cameron of Pennsylvania. It was because of his conservative tendencies, that these three leaders formed the purpose to bring Grant again to the Presidency. Yet the Hayes Administration was not always conservative, and many believed that its moderation had afforded a much-needed breathing spell to the country. Towards its close all became better satisfied, the radical portion by the President's later efforts to prevent the intimidation of negro voters in the South—a form of intimidation which was now accomplished by means of rifle clubs, still another advance from the White League and the Ku-Klux. He made this a leading feature in his Message to the Congress in 1878, and by an abandonment of his earlier policy he succeeded in reuniting what were then fast-separating wings of his own party.

In his last annual Message, in December, 1880, in

RUTHERFORD B. HAYES.

the course of a lengthy discussion of the civil service, the President declared that, in his opinion, "every citizen has an equal right to the honor and profit of entering the public service of his country.

The only just ground of discrimination is the measure of character and capacity he has to make that service most useful to the people. Except in cases where, upon just and recognized principles, as upon the theory of pensions, offices and promotions are bestowed as rewards for past services, their bestowal upon any theory which disregards personal merit is an act of injustice to the citizen, as well as a breach of that trust subject to which the appointing power is held."

In pursuance of his reform of the Civil Service, he removed Chester A. Arthur (afterwards Vice-President and President), from his office of Collector at New York City. This is the most valued office under the administration, and Arthur was the particular friend of Senator Conkling, and a firm believer in, and upholder of, the old political adage that "to the victor belongs the spoils."

The effect of his administration was, in a political sense, to strengthen a growing independent sentiment in the ranks of the Republicans—an element more conservative generally in its views than those represented by Conkling and Blaine. This sentiment began with Bristow, who while in the Cabinet made a show of seeking out and punishing all corruptions in Government office or service. On this platform and record he had contested with Hayes the honors of the Presidential nominations, and while the latter was at the time believed to well represent the same views, they were not urgently pressed during his administration. Indeed, without the knowledge of Hayes, what was said to be a most gigantic "steal," under the name of the Star Route bills, had its birth, and thrived so well that no important discovery was made until the incoming of the Garfield Administration. The Hayes Administration, it is now fashionable to say, made little impress for good or evil upon the country, but impartial historians will give it the credit of softening party asperities and aiding very materially in the restoration of better feeling between the North and South. Its conservatism, always manifested save on extraordinary occasions, did that much good at least. He was active in pressing forward the resumption of specie payments.

He died on January 17, 1893, and was buried at Columbus, Ohio.

The Republicans met, June 5, 1880, at Chicago. The excitement in the ranks of the Republicans was very high, because of the candidacy of Grant for what was popularly called a "third term," though not a third consecutive term. His friends, in the face of bitter protests, had secured the instructions of their respective State Conventions for Grant. Conkling had done this in New York, Cameron in Pennsylvania, Logan in Illinois. Still there was a large minority in the delegations of these States opposed to his nomination. The convention was in session three days. The following was the vote on the first ballot: Grant, 304; Blaine, 284; Sherman, 93; Edmunds, 34; Washburne, 30; Windom, 10. On the second ballot, Garfield and Harrison each received one vote. The vote remained about the same for three days, when it got to be "anything to beat Grant."

The prejudice against a third term is unyielding.

It is more than sentiment. It is wisdom. Experience has burned this precaution in the public mind. Great power must frequently be recalled by the people and transferred to new hands. And so Grant was called down.

James A. Garfield, of Ohio, was nominated on the 36th ballot, Grant's forces alone remaining solid. After Garfield's nomination there was a temporary adjournment, during which the friends of the nominee consulted Conkling and his leading friends, and the result was the selection of Chester A. Arthur of New York for Vice-President. The object of this selection was to carry New York, the great State which was then believed to hold the key to the Presidential position.

The Democrats met at Cincinnati, June 22, 1880. Tilden had, up to the holding of the Pennsylvania State Convention, been the most promising candidate. There was a struggle between the Wallace and Randall factions of Pennsylvania, the former favoring Hancock, the latter Tilden. Wallace won, and bound the delegation by the unit rule. When the convention met, John Kelly, the Tammany leader of New York, was again there, as at St. Louis, four years before, to oppose Tilden, but the latter sent a letter disclaiming that he was a candidate, and yet really inviting a nomination on the issue of "the fraudulent counting in of Hayes." There were but two ballots. On the first ballot, the "favorite sons" of the several States received the customary complimentary vote. On the first ballot Hancock received 171 votes; Bayard, 153½; and Tilden, 38.

On the second ballot Hancock received 705, Tilden 1, Hendricks 30.

Thus General Winfield Scott Hancock, of New York, was nominated on the second ballot. William H. English, of Indiana, was nominated for Vice-President.

The Greenback-Labor Convention nominated General J. B. Weaver, of Iowa, for President; and General E. J. Chambers, of Texas, for Vice-President.

In the canvass which followed, the Republican orators visited the October States of Ohio and Indiana, as it was believed that these would determine the result, Maine having in September very unexpectedly defeated the Republican State ticket by a small majority. Conkling held aloof at first. It was believed that Hancock's splendid military record would carry him through, and it was absolutely necessary to do something to offset this popularity. Great influences were brought to bear on Conkling for assistance. With Grant, he swung around the circle of States, making a "business" campaign of it; predicting all manner of direful things if a change were made in the administration of affairs. The "business" vote settled it. Garfield was elected.

General Hancock made the great blunder of saying that the "tariff was a purely local issue." This sentence cost him Pennsylvania.

Every issue was recalled, but for the first time in the history of the Republicans of the West, they accepted the tariff issue, and made open war on the plank in the Democratic platform—"a tariff for revenue only." Iowa, Ohio, and Indiana all elected the

Republican State tickets with good margins; West Virginia went Democratic, but the result was, notwithstanding this, reasonably assured to the Repub-

GENERAL W. S. HANCOCK.

licans. The Democrats, however, feeling the strong personal popularity of their leading candidate, persisted with high courage to the end. In November all of the Southern States, with New Jersey, California, and Nevada in the North, went Democratic; all of the others, Republican. The Greenbackers held only a balance of power, which they could not exercise, in California, Indiana, and New Jersey. The electoral vote of Garfield and Arthur was 214; that of Hancock and English, 155. The popular vote was: Republican, 4,442,950; Democratic, 4,442,035; Greenback or National, 306,867; scattering, 12,576. The Congressional elections in the same canvass gave the Republicans 147 members, the Democrats, 136; Greenbackers, 9; Independents, 1.

JAMES A. GARFIELD—1881 (200 days).

JAMES ABRAM GARFIELD, the twentieth President, was born in Ohio, November 19, 1831, of Puritan ancestors. His father died soon after the birth of James, leaving a widow and four small children in poor circumstances. He knew what deprivation and poverty meant. When he was ten years old he did such work as he could on the neighboring farms, chopping wood, and driving horses on the tow-path of a canal, and drudging generally; and spent his winters at the district school. In 1849 he joined the Campbellites, a religious offshoot from the Baptists. He went through Hiram College, in Ohio, supporting himself by teaching, and graduated at Williams College, in Massachusetts, in 1856.

Returning to Hiram College, which was a Campbellite institution, he became its president, and there began studying law. He was elected to the State Senate in 1859; and when the war began he was

JAMES ABRAM GARFIELD.

placed in command of a regiment of volunteers. In 1862 he was made a brigadier-general, and was promoted to be a major-general for gallantry at

Chickamauga. He shortly after resigned his command to enter Congress. He remained in Congress till 1880, where he rendered valuable service on military and financial questions. In January, 1880, he was elected to the United States Senate; and in June of the same year he was nominated for the Presidency on the Republican ticket. His nomination was a surprise, and the result of a fusion of the friends of Sherman and Blaine to defeat Grant. He delivered speeches in his own behalf during the campaign (an unprecedented performance up to this time), and defeated General Hancock, his Democratic opponent, by a very narrow majority on the popular vote, but by 214 to 155 on the electoral vote. James B. Weaver, the Greenbacker and Labor candidate, polled 307,306 votes; and there were over 10,000 votes cast for the Prohibition ticket.

James A. Garfield was inaugurated President on March 4, 1881. His address promised full and equal protection of the Constitution and the laws for the negro, advocated universal education as a safeguard of suffrage, and recommended such an adjustment of our monetary system "that the purchasing power of every coined dollar will be exactly equal to its debt-paying power in all the markets of the world." The national debt should be refunded at a lower rate of interest, without compelling the withdrawal of the National Bank notes; polygamy should be prohibited, and civil service regulated by law.

James G. Blaine was made Secretary of State; William Windom, of Minnesota, Secretary of the Treasury; and Robert T. Lincoln, of Illinois, a son of the martyred President), Secretary of War.

The parties were even in this session of the Senate and Vice-President Arthur had to employ the casting vote on all questions where the parties divided; he invariably cast it on the side of the Republicans.

The President nominated William H. Robertson, the leader of the Blaine wing of the party in New York, to be Collector of Customs. Conkling unsuccessfully fought this nomination with all his power and influence, but Robertson was eventually confirmed.

These events widely separated the factions in New York—one wing calling itself "Stalwart," the other "Half-Breed," a term of contempt flung at the Independents by Conkling. Conkling and his associate, Thomas C. Platt, resigned from the Senate. Elections followed to fill the vacancies, the New York Legislature being in session. It was confidently assumed that both Conkling and Platt would be immediately returned. This would give Conkling the endorsement of his State in his opposition to the administration. Vice-President Arthur worked indefatigably but unavailingly in his effort to bring Conkling's renomination around. These vacancies gave the Democrats for the time control of the U. S. Senate, but they thought it unwise to pursue an advantage which would compel them to show their hands for or against one or other of the opposing Republican factions. Warner A. Miller became Platt's successor, and Elbridge G. Lapham was elected to fill Conkling's place.

On the morning of Saturday, July 2, 1881, Garfield accompanied by Blaine, left the Executive Mansion to take a train for New England, where he intended to visit the college from which he had graduated. He was walking through the main waiting-room, when Charles J. Guiteau, a persistent and disappointed office-seeker, entered through the main door, and fired two shots, one of which took fatal effect. The bullet striking the President about four inches to the right of the spinal column, struck the tenth and badly shattered the eleventh rib. The shock to the President's system was very severe, and at first apprehensions were felt that death would ensue speedily. Two hours after the shooting he was removed to the Executive Mansion and from thence to Long Branch, where, in a cottage at Elberon, it was hoped vigor would return. At first, indications justified the most sanguine expectations, but he died at 10.35 on the night of September 19, 1881, and our nation mourned, as it had only done once before, when Abraham Lincoln also fell by the hand of an assassin. Guiteau was tried, convicted, and hung, the jury rejecting his plea of insanity.

Once again was the country draped in mourning as the body of the second assassinated President passed through the land to its final resting-place in Cleveland.

At midnight on September 19, the Cabinet telegraphed to Vice-President Arthur to take the oath of office, and this he very properly did before a local judge. He was soon afterwards again sworn in at Washington, with the usual ceremonies. He requested the Cabinet to hold on until Congress met, and it would have remained intact had Secretary Windom not found it necessary to resume his place in the Senate.

CHESTER A. ARTHUR—1881–1885.

CHESTER ALAN ARTHUR, who became our twenty-first President, on the assassination of James A. Garfield, was born in Vermont, October 5, 1830. His father was a Baptist minister and a native of the North of Ireland. He distinguished himself as a student at Union College, New York, and devoting himself to law studies, was admitted to the bar in 1853. At the beginning of the Civil War he held the post of inspector-general, and during the war he was quarter-master-general for the New York forces. He took a prominent share in politics on the Republican side, and in 1871, General Grant appointed him Collector of Customs at the port of New York, a very much coveted post. As being hostile to the reform in the civil service aimed at by President Hayes, he was removed from this post in 1878. He was the leader of the Republican party in New York State, and though belonging to the section of the party opposed to civil service reform to that represented by Garfield he was made the Vice-President when Garfield became President in 1881. Garfield's death called him to the supreme magistracy of the Union. He was provisionally inaugurated at midnight on September 19, 1881, on notice of Garfield's death. He was formally sworn into the office later at Washington with the customary ceremonies.

One of his law cases that first brought him into notoriety in New York City was the winning of a suit in 1856, giving blacks the right to ride on the horse cars. Some of the cars at that time bore the curious legend, "Colored people allowed to ride in these cars."

He brought to his Cabinet as Secretary of State, T. F. Freylinghuysen, of New Jersey. For Secretary of the Treasury he appointed Charles J. Folger, of New York, and upon his death, soon after taking the office, it was conferred upon Walter Q. Gresham, of Illinois. He offered Senator Conkling a seat in the Supreme Court, but it was declined. He signed the anti-polygamy bill, March 23, 1882.

In person Arthur was tall, large, well-proportioned, and of distinguished presence. His manners were affable. He was genial in domestic and social life, and warmly liked by his personal friends.

General Arthur's was a quiet, clean, and business-like administration. He succeeded in checking the divisions in his party, and retired on March 4, 1885, with the good will of the entire country. In this respect he differed from all the preceding "accidental" Presidents, like Tyler, Fillmore, and Johnson. He died suddenly of apoplexy in New York City, November 18, 1886, and was buried at Albany, New York.

The Chinese Question was settled during this administration. Since 1877 there had been a constant agitation in California, and other States and Territories on the Pacific slope, for the prohibition of Chinese immigration, which they regarded in the light of an invasion.

President Hayes vetoed the first bill interdicting such immigration on the ground that it was a "violation of the spirit of treaty stipulations."

On February 28, 1882, a new bill was offered in

the Senate prohibiting immigration to Chinese or Coolie laborers for a period of 20 years. Senator John F. Miller, who fathered the bill and who was

CHESTER ALAN ARTHUR.

conversant with all the leading facts in the history of the agitation, in explaining this antipathy said: "It has been said that the advocates of Chinese restriction were to be found only among the vicious, unlettered foreign element of California society. To show the fact in respect of this contention, the Legislature of California in 1878 provided for a vote of the people upon the question of Chinese immigration (so called) to be had at the general election of 1879. The vote was legally taken, without excitement, and the response was general. When the ballots were counted, there were found to be 883 votes for Chinese immigration and 154,638 against it. A similar vote was taken in Nevada and resulted as follows: 183 votes for Chinese immigration and 17,259 votes against."

Senator Jones, of Nevada, supported the bill and in resisting the fallacy that cheap labor produces national wealth called attention to the home condition of the 350,000,000 Chinese.

The bill passed the Senate by a 29 to 15 vote, and passed the House, March 23, 1882, by 167 favoring votes to 65 negative votes, and receiving the approval of Arthur became a law.

In 1884, the Republican Convention met at Chicago. The candidates for nomination were: Chester A. Arthur, of New York ; James G. Blaine, of Maine; John Sherman, of Ohio; George F. Edmunds, of Vermont; John A. Logan, of Illinois; and Joseph R. Hawley, of Connecticut. The convention sat for four days, and balloted as follows:

	1st Ballot.	2d.	3d.	4th.
Blaine	334	349	375	541
Arthur	278	275	274	207
Edmunds	93	85	96	41
Logan	63	61	53	7
Sherman	30	28	25	—

There were 820 votes. Blaine and Logan received the nominations for President and Vice-President.

In this convention, President Arthur stood out

JAMES G. BLAINE.

for the nomination as his due, and as a vindication of the clean and dignified administration he had given the country after Garfield's death. Gresham, who was Arthur's Secretary of the Treasury, was approached about his candidacy, but he insisted that under no circumstances would he allow his name to be used as long as Arthur desired the nomination. He was loyal to his chief, and did all that he could to promote his chances to succeed himself. But it was not to be.

The Democrats also met in Chicago. Opposition was manifested to the unit rule. An effort was made to abolish the two-thirds rule, but this was met with such decided disfavor that it was abandoned.

The prominent nominees were: Grover Cleveland, of New York; Thomas F. Bayard, of Delaware; Allen G. Thurman, of Ohio; and Samuel J. Randall, of Pennsylvania. There were only two ballots taken. On the first, Cleveland had 392 votes, Bayard, 168, Thurman 88, Randall 78, and there were about 90 scattering votes. On the second ballot, Grover Cleveland received 684 votes (547 being necessary), and he was therefore declared the nominee for the Presidency. Thomas A. Hendricks, of Indiana, was given the nomination for Vice-President.

The People's and Greenback ticket nominated Benjamin F. Butler, who polled 133,880 votes, thus aiding the Blaine ticket; but as an offset to this, the Prohibition ticket polled 150,633 votes, nearly all of which were pulled from the Republican nominees. Grover Cleveland was elected President, receiving 219 electoral votes, while Blaine polled but 182 votes. On the popular vote, Cleveland had a plurality of nearly 63,000 votes.

This was probably the most exciting canvass in the history of American politics. Fiery enthusiasm on both sides was everywhere displayed, and both parties indulged in the hottest kind of partisanship. The personal character of both the Presidential

GENERAL BENJAMIN F. BUTLER.

nominees were rancorously assailed. It was a veritable campaign of mud. Blaine and Logan made tours around the country. Blaine was followed by reporters and shadowed by detectives in the hope that he might be betrayed into some expression that could be used against him or tortured into helping his opponents. He had almost got to the end, and would unquestionably have been elected, but for one miserable mishap—or, as was claimed, a trick that was sprung upon him on the Thursday preceding the election.

Blaine was in New York, and among the many delegations visiting him was one of 300 ministers, who wished to show their confidence in his moral and intellectual fitness for the Chief Magistracy. The oldest of the ministers present was Mr. Burchard, and he was assigned to deliver the address. In closing it, he referred to what he thought ought to be a common opposition to "Rum, Romanism, and Rebellion"—an alliteration which not only awakened the wrath of the Democracy, but which quickly estranged many of the Irish-American supporters of Blaine and Logan.

Blaine on the two following days tried to counteract the effects of an imprudence for which he was in no way responsible, but the alliteration was instantly and everywhere employed to revive religious issues and hatreds, and to such an extent that circulars were distributed at the doors of Catholic churches, implying that Blaine himself had used the offensive words. It was placarded all along the New York State canals. A more unexpected blow was never known in our political history. It determined the result. It changed New York's 36 electoral votes and gave Cleveland the Presidency.

GROVER CLEVELAND— $\begin{cases} 1885-1889. \\ 1893-1897. \end{cases}$

STEPHEN GROVER CLEVELAND, our twenty-second, and twenty-fourth President, was born in New Jersey, on March 18, 1837. His father was a Presbyterian minister, who moved into New York when Grover was about three years old. The father died, leaving his widow with five children, and in poor circumstances. He first clerked in a store. In 1859 he was admitted to the bar, and started practising in Buffalo. When the war broke out, it is said he desired to enlist, but he was dissuaded by the idea that some one should stay at home and look after the family. Two of his brothers went off to the front. He was drafted, but the State provided a substitute. From 1863 to 1866 he was Assistant District Attorney for Erie County. He rose to be Sheriff, and subsequently Mayor of Buffalo. In 1882, aided by a united party and the hearty support of the independent press of the State, he was elected Governor by a sweeping majority. His administration of the office satisfied everybody. In 1884 he was the Democratic nominee for the Presidency, and after a most exciting canvass was elected, receiving 219 electoral votes, while his opponent, Blaine, received but 182 votes. He was inaugurated March 4, 1885, and served his term of four years.

In 1888, Cleveland was unanimously renominated; but he was this time defeated by Benjamin Harrison. In 1892 he was again placed at the head of the Democratic ticket with President Harrison again his opponent; and, after a very close canvass, he was once more elected; and once more, on March 4, 1893, he took the oath at Washington to "faithfully execute the office of President."

In his first term, Thomas F. Bayard, of Delaware, was appointed Secretary of State; and Daniel Manning of New York was placed in charge of the Treasury. Manning was a very able man; he was greatly instrumental in securing the nomination for Cleveland, and subsequently very active in electing him.

This (1885-1889) was the first Democratic administration in 24 years. The politicians were naturally hungry for office, and raised the cry, "Turn the rascals out." The President ignored this clamor, and declared that "public office was a public trust," and in consequence there would be no wholesale dismissals. This was not particularly cheering to the rank and file, who had walked the wilderness for a quarter of a century; and it was the occasion of widespread dissatisfaction within his party.

The efforts of the first administration were directed towards appeasing civic wranglings and holding a close political alliance with the Civil Service reformers, without disrupting the party by totally refusing to distribute the spoils of office. Things went along smoothly till the meeting of Congress in 1887, when, instead of the customary Message dealing with the foreign relations of the nation, Cleveland precipitated a surprising address on the Tariff question, dealing with our domestic affairs. This address was forced into such prominence in the ensuing Presidential campaign, that it became the single issue.

The Democrats met in St. Louis, on June 5, 1888, and were in session three days. The President's last

Message and the Mills Tariff Bill were endorsed. This result was not satisfying to the Protective Tariff Democrats, but they were without any courageous representation and the Platform was adopted with but one dissenting vote. Grover Cleveland was renominated by acclamation. The Vice-Presidential nomination went to Allen G. Thurman.

The Republicans met at Chicago, on June 19, 1888. Blaine was up in all the ballots, and it was within the power of his friends to nominate him: but his final refusal led them to vote for Benjamin Harrison of Indiana. Levi P. Morton, of New York, was nominated for Vice-President. The voting opened with 229 votes for John Sherman, of Ohio; W. Q. Gresham received 111 votes; Harrison received 80 votes on the first ballot, then rose to 298, and on the eighth ballot received 544 votes.

The Republicans accepted in the plainest way the issues thus thrust upon the country by Cleveland's Message. Visiting delegates from both parties went through all the great States, enthusing their respective partisans.

The election resulted in Harrison receiving 233 electoral votes. Cleveland got but 168 votes. Harrison and Morton were therefore elected, and took their offices on March 4, 1889.

During Cleveland's first term, four States were admitted into the Union on February 22, 1889: North Dakota, South Dakota, Montana, and Washington.

[For the incidents surrounding the subsequent, or 1893 campaign, see under Harrison.]

Grover Cleveland was inaugurated as our twenty-fourth President on March 4, 1893. To his Cabinet

GROVER CLEVELAND.

he called Walter Q. Gresham, of Illinois (a Republican), as Secretary of State; Senator John G. Carlisle, of Kentucky, was placed at the head of the

Treasury Department. Richard S. Olney, of Massachusetts, was appointed Attorney-General. Gresham died in 1895, and Olney was advanced to the office of Secretary of State.

Cleveland's first act, on March 4, 1893, was to request the Senate to recall the Treaty of Annexation with Hawaii—one of the last acts of the Harrison Administration, just before Cleveland's accession. On April 14, the American Protectorate established there was withdrawn by Commissioner Blount, who had gone there as the President's direct representative. Cleveland tried unsuccessfully to reinstate the dethroned Queen, but was thwarted by the Revolutionists, who would not have her. The Republic of Hawaii was proclaimed on July 4, 1893. On August 9, it was officially recognized by us.

During Cleveland's second administration was celebrated the 400th anniversary of the discovery of America by Columbus. A "Columbian" Exposition was carried on in Chicago for six months, from May till November, 1893. It was the *greatest* exposition ever held in the world. Its beauty was simply marvelous. The receipts for admission were nearly eleven millions of dollars, which will convey some impression of its magnitude, and of the furore it occasioned at home and abroad. The buildings cost nearly thirty millions of dollars; they were built on Lake Michigan and styled the "White City." The exposition was visited by nearly twenty-eight million people.

On November 7, 1893, eleven States held elections. The Democrats carried Virginia, Kentucky, and Maryland. The Republicans got the rebound of the "tidal wave," and polled surprisingly large majorities from the great manufacturing States of New York, New Jersey, Pennsylvania, Massachusetts; and from Ohio, Indiana, Nebraska and South Dakota. In other words, the Administration carried three States, with a voting representation of 417,267 votes; while the Republicans carried eight States, represented by nearly 3,000,000 votes.

William McKinley, the father of the "McKinley Tariff Bill," was elected Governor of Ohio by a very large majority over L. T. Neal, his Democratic opponent, and the author of the "Protection is a Fraud" plank in the 1892 Cleveland Platform.

In the summer of 1893 a money panic was provoked by the banks who refused the customary discounting accommodations to the business community, no matter how financially stable they might have been. They attributed the "panic" to the "Silver Purchasing Act," and the President convened a special Congress to consider the crisis. After a long and acrimonious debate, in which all free coinage amendments were rejected, the Silver Repeal Act was passed, October 30, 1893, many Republicans voting with the Democrats.

On December 19, 1893, a tariff bill known as the "Wilson Bill" was offered in the House. It was debated for 23 days, and passed February 1, 1894. It went to the Senate, where it was debated till July, and after numerous conferences and amendments was finally passed by a strict party vote, 182 being for, and 106 against the measure. The House agreed to the bill on August 13, 1894.

The bill was not satisfactory to the President, who insisted on free raw materials. He allowed it to become a law without his approval.

An "Income Tax" provision was inserted in the bill at the President's suggestion. He claimed that it would be paid by millionaires without falling on any of them oppressively. The press rancorously assailed the constitutionality of the law. It struggled through the House, and won its way through a reluctant Senate. It was voted for by 172 Democrats and 10 Populists. There were but 48 votes against it, these being mainly Republicans. The U. S. Supreme Court subsequently decided that the Income Tax was unconstitutional, and it became inoperative. It was confidently expected by the President and his following that the bill would have been sustained by the court. Its being thrown out reduced the revenues of the Government more than 30 millions of dollars; and obliged the President to beg from Congress the authority to issue gold bonds —in other words—to borrow enough money to cover the deficiency forced upon the Government by the changed conditions of our tariff laws.

In a nut-shell the case resolves itself to this: President Harrison in four years reduced the national debt $236,527,666; President Cleveland in three years increased the interest-bearing bonded debt $262,602,245. If the Wilson Tariff Bill as it first passed the House, where it met with the hearty approval of the President, had become law, the deficiency in revenue would have been much greater.

An act enabling Utah to enter the Union was enacted, and on January 4, 1896, she made the 45th State, and added another star to the national flag.

The elections of November, 1894, resulted in great Republican victories. 21 States elected governors, and of these only three elected Democrats. The elections of 1895 resulted in even greater Republican victories. Elections were held in 12 States and all but one were carried by the Republicans, generally by large majorities. The solitary Democratic State was Mississippi.

No great party was ever so sweepingly repudiated as the Democratic organization has been during the past three years. The elections of 1893, 1894, 1895, all showed that the country profoundly regretted the blunder of 1892. As Representative Cannon of Illinois succinctly put it, "Ever since the Democratic administration came into power there has been deficiency, distress, idleness, and panic."

The Cuban Revolution began on February 20, 1895, by uprisings in different parts of the island. It has continued with various results ever since. The previous uprising lasted from 1878 till 1888, when the Cubans surrendered upon promises from Spain of reforms that have never been accorded. The Senate and House passed resolutions favoring the recognition of belligerency, and calling upon the Executive to expostulate with Spain and prevent her treating her rebellious subjects as brigands or pirates. The President treated these resolutions as if they were a precipitate and perfunctory expression of ephemeral opinion; and did everything in his power to aid Spain in maintaining her despotic and destructive sovereignty over Cuba.

The Venezuela case was originally a boundary question. Discoveries of gold in Venezuela and the growing importance of the Orinoco River, led the British to claim that the boundary of British Guiana extends to the Orinoco, and included these gold fields. Our Government recommended arbitration to settle the question; but Great Britain, having a bad case, refused to accede. When British subjects entered the disputed territory, they were arrested by the Venezuelans, and for this Great Britain demanded an indemnity. She threatened to seize a part of Venezuela to enforce her demands; and the President surprised the public by nobly championing the cause of little Venezuela as against Great Britain, on the ground that our Monroe Doctrine would not allow us to entertain the idea of any foreign government possessing any portion of this continent—either by grab or purchase. Lord Salisbury refused peremptorily to arbitrate the question, but six months later England accepted the solution proposed by the United States.

The world was surprised at the unanimity with which the President's Venezuelan Message was endorsed by the people, who showed that they were strong, prepared, and thoroughly united.

The Republicans met in St. Louis, on June 16, 1896. Two days were spent in formulating the platform. Governor William McKinley, of Ohio, received on the first ballot $661\frac{1}{2}$ votes, and was therefore nominated with an unanimity not expressed for any successful new candidate, with the exception of Fremont, the first Republican candidate in 1856, and Grant, the third, in 1868. They alone were nominated for a first term on the first ballot. Garret A. Hobart, of New Jersey, received the Vice-Presidential nomination. The platform was staunchly Republican.

The Democratic Convention met at Chicago, July 7, and on the 10th, it nominated, on the fifth ballot, William J. Bryan, of Nebraska, for President, and Arthur Sewall, of Maine, for the second place on the ticket. The Convention was under the full control of the Silverites, and they dominated its action. The sound money Democrats, as they styled themselves, openly revolted against silver, and demanded a new ticket. Whitney and Hill and other prominent Democrats were pronounced in their hostility to the Chicago platform and ticket, and the *New York Sun* came out distinctly for McKinley, advising all sound-money and other Democrats to so vote as the only means of defeating the Bryan programme, which it denounced as a compound of plunder, anarchy and repudiation.

The Cleveland administration felt exceedingly sore over the outcome. They objected to the "regular" nominee, and still could not persuade themselves to vote for McKinley, who was heralded as "the apostle of protection and the advance agent of prosperity." A third ticket was accordingly placed in the field on September 3, by the sound money Democrats placing in nomination General John M. Palmer, of Illinois, and General Simon B. Buckner, of Kentucky. This alliance of the "blue and the gray" was intended to attract those Democrats who might, in the absence of the third ticket, vote for Bryan and Sewall. Cleveland endorsed this ticket and the "old" Democracy.

The Populists nominated the Vice-President first, naming Thomas E. Watson, of Georgia; and then endorsed Bryan for the Presidency. Watson received 52,000 votes, or 20,000 more than the Palmer ticket.

The contest for the presidency was the most tremendous contest of years. The McKinleyites were supported by nearly all the most influential newspapers. They controlled an abundant campaign fund which was lavishly expended. The Bryanites had barely funds to meet necessary expenses. Bryan showed himself to be the strongest candidate his party could have chosen. He is a very able, determined, clear-headed man, of the golden age of 36, and in the future movements of his party he will have to be considered as a very important factor. Had the general election taken place in August, Bryan might possibly have been elected. Certainly there was more study of true politics in this country during the last half of 1896 than previously in thirty years. By October the pendulum of public opinion had swung back, and the feeling was that McKinley would be unquestionably elected, but by a slender majority.

Great was the consternation of the Bryanites, and the jubilation of the Republicans, at the unprecedented majorities rolled up for McKinley, whose election was secured by a plurality of over one million of the popular vote—the largest ever given.

BENJAMIN HARRISON—1889-1893.

BENJAMIN HARRISON, our twenty-third President, was born in Ohio, August 20, 1833, and was one of a family of nine children. His father was a son of President William Henry Harrison. Benjamin graduated from Miami University, Ohio, in 1852. He studied law and settled in Indianapolis, Indiana, to practise his profession in 1854. When the war broke out he raised a company of volunteers and was its second lieutenant, from which he rose to a Colonelcy. He served in the Atlanta campaigns under Sherman and distinguished himself at the battle of Resaca. He took part in the battle of Nashville under General Thomas in 1864. In 1865 he was made a brevet-Brigadier-General.

He took an active part in Grant's Presidential campaign in 1868 and again in 1872. In 1876 he ran for Governor of Indiana, but was defeated. He declined a Cabinet office under Garfield. He was elected to the U. S. Senate in 1880, but was defeated when he ran for re-election six years later. In 1888, he was the Republican nominee for the Presidency against Grover Cleveland, and was elected. He was sworn into office March 4, 1889.

James G. Blaine was called to the Cabinet as Secretary of State; and William Windom was made Secretary of the Treasury. Secretary Windom died January 29, 1891, and was followed in the office by Charles Foster, of Ohio. John Wanamaker, of Philadelphia, was Postmaster-General.

In December, 1889, the McKinley Tariff Bill was

passed. Its main features were a large reduction in revenues caused by a substantial removal of duties from raw sugar, a sytem of bounties for sugar grown here, an increase of duty on many manufactured articles, and the adoption of a clause suggested by Blaine favoring reciprocity with other American Nations. Wyoming and Idaho were admitted as States.

The Republicans met at Minneapolis, June 7, 1892. Blaine had written the Chairman of the Convention that his name would not be presented as a candidate. Harrison's re-nomination was opposed by the political leaders in New York, Pennsylvania, Ohio, Iowa, Louisiana, Colorado, Oregon, and Missouri, who agreed to present and support Blaine, feeling satisfied he would accept if his nomination was plainly for the good of the party. The feeling against "boss" rule, as it was styled, prevented Blaine's nomination. McKinley, the father of the 1890 Tariff bill, was suggested, but he voted for Harrison and resisted the proposed stampede in his favor. Thereupon Harrison was re-nominated, receiving 535 votes to 182 each for both McKinley and Blaine. Whitelaw Reid, of New York, was placed on the ticket for the Vice-Presidency, in the place of Levi P. Morton.

The Democrats met at Chicago, June 21, 1892. Cleveland was the avowed nominee. He was opposed by Senator David B. Hill and the whole power of Tammany Hall in New York City, who repeatedly declared that he could not carry his own State. Balloting was reached on the 23d, at four o'clock in the morning, the Cleveland leaders, under

W. C. Whitney, doing this to prevent combinations by the opposition. Cleveland received 617 votes;

BENJAMIN HARRISON.

David B. Hill, 115; Governor Boies, of Iowa, 103; with 75 scattering. Cleveland was thereupon unanimously renominated. Adlai E. Stevenson, of Illinois, was nominated for the Vice-Presidency on the first ballot.

A notable scene in the convention was created when a radical free-trade plank was moved as a substitute for the more moderate utterances of the platform. The substitute denounced the protective tariff as a fraud. It was reported that the substitute was prepared by the Anti-Cleveland leaders. The result of the vote was 564 for the substitute, and 314 against it.

The campaign was run on about the same general issues as in 1888. Harrison, however, was considerably weakened by the substitution of Reid for Vice-President, in place of Morton. Reid was strenuously objected to by all the labor-unions in the country. His candidacy cost Harrison the vote of New York, and thereby a re-election. He had carried the State in 1889 by 14,000 plurality.

Cleveland and Stevenson received 277 electoral votes, and Harrison and Reid but 145. On the popular vote, Cleveland received 98,017 more than Harrison.

Ex-President Hayes and James G. Blaine died in January, 1893.

In Hawaii, the queen was dethroned by the revolutionists, and on February 1st Minister Stevens raised the United States flag at Honolulu, landed the U. S. marines, and established a protectorate. A treaty of annexation to the United States was about to be signed, but the President thought it a matter of courtesy to hold over all further proceedings for action by his successor. A bad thing, as it turned out, for Cleveland tried in every conceivable way to recognize the monarchy, and reinstate the deposed queen.

Although General Harrison's term was distinguished by no very remarkable events, yet a large number of useful measures were adopted, and a model of executive administration was presented. There was vigilance in the execution of the law by all its officers and guardians. There was no waste; no stealing; no defalcations, and there was no rings nor jobs. There was probity and integrity in office; there was no purchasing of votes or corrupt means practised to influence legislation; there was public and private virtue; at the courts of foreign nations we were represented by men of experience, learning and ability.

On the inauguration of Cleveland and Stevenson, General Harrison returned to Indianapolis, Indiana, and resumed the practice of the law.

The national debt was reduced during this administration $236,527,666; a very repectable showing.

[The more important of the measures of the *second* Cleveland Administration will be found in the preceding pages under Cleveland.]

WILLIAM McKINLEY—1897-1901.

William McKinley, our twenty-fifth President, was born at Niles, Ohio, on January, 29, 1843. He was educated at the public schools; enlisted in an Ohio regiment, at the age of eighteen, and served through the Civil War, attaining the rank of Captain and Brevet-Major. He was admitted to the bar in 1867; served as a member of Congress from 1887 to 1891, when he was jerrymandered out of his seat; he was Chairman of the Committee of Ways and Means, which framed the tariff of 1890—known as the McKinley Bill. He was elected Governor of Ohio in 1891, and again in 1893. He has now reached the highest office in the gift of the people.

Governor McKinley was duly inaugurated President; Lyman J. Gage, a banker in Chicago, was placed in charge of the Treasury Department; Russell A. Alger, of Michigan, was made Secretary of War; John D. Long, of Massachusetts, was placed at the head of the Navy; Joseph McKenna, of California, was made Attorney General, but was subsequently elevated to the United States Supreme Court, and John W. Griggs, of New Jersey, was appointed in his stead. Senator John Sherman, of Ohio was made Secretary of State. He retired in April, 1898, and his office was turned over to William R. Day, of Ohio, who had served as Assistant Secretary. He was appointed one of the Spanish Peace Commissioners, and the office was conferred on John Hay, another Ohioan, who had been Minister at London.

Repeated efforts had been made by Congress during the Cleveland administration to recognize the belligerency of the Cubans in the war with Spain. These efforts were all quietly ignored by the president and his secretary (Olney). Reports continued to reach us of the heart-sickening condition of the starving people whom Weyler, the Spanish general, had driven from their farm homes into the cities, where there was no employment for them, no provision made for their maintenance in this barbaric captivity. These forced the Cuban situation upon the consciences of all true Americans. Its immediate effect was fol-

WILLIAM MCKINLEY.

lowed by an exchange of notes between our government and Spain, followed by Spain's offer of autonomy, and more liberty to Cuba than that government ever before granted to any of its dependencies. Autonomy was repudiated by the Cubans, who declared, "We are fighting for liberty ; not for reforms."

These promised reforms were intended simply to delude for a time the people of the United States. The scheme was an extremely adroit one, and nothing more shamelessly mendacious was ever attempted. McKinley was surrounded by advocates of peace who had been opposing the war on constitutional, philanthropic, or religious grounds. He wished to avoid war, and was imposed upon by these stratagems, until an intercepted or stolen letter from the Spanish minister to a friend in Havana betrayed the fact that Spain was simply jollying this country, and figuring for delay. De Lome in this letter characterized the president as a " low politician," and expressed the belief that he " could manipulate things in Washington to suit the exigencies of Spain." Our government demanded his instant recall.

The Spanish government exhausted all the arts of diplomacy in figuring for delay. The Pope and the European powers were influenced to intervene. However much they sympathized with Spain, they were arrested by prudential considerations from interfering. England, contrary to her old-time attitude, showed herself decidedly friendly throughout, and there was a strong suspicion that some secret agreement had been reached between the two nations.

Fitzhugh Lee had been to Havana as Consul General, and Murat Halstead, a well-known and trained journalist went there in a semi-official capacity. Later on Senator Proctor, of Vermont visited the island. They all denounced Spanish misrule there as worse than anything they had ever known about. Cuba had been reduced by Spanish atrocity from a land of plenty to a howling wilderness. The Spaniards had sent across the Atlantic more than 200,000 of their sons to fight against Cuban rebels, and more than half of these were killed or hopelessly disabled. Cuba on her part seems to have lost nearly half the population of the island.

McKinley proffered upon purely humanitarian grounds to relieve the starving *reconcentrados* in Cuba, but this was not kindly received by public opinion in Spain, and was resented by the Spanish government on the ground that it was the entering wedge for American intervention.

To establish a feeling of fairness and friendliness between the two nations an interchange of naval visits was suggested. The announcement was received by the Spanish government with apparent pleasure, and

ADMIRAL DEWEY.

the battleship "Maine" was ordered to call at the port of Havana, and was taken and moored by the government pilot to an anchorage assigned by the authorities; the harbor being for a good while under absolute military control.

The "Maine" with her officers and crew numbered about 400. She reached Havana on January 20th, 1898, and on the evening of February 15th she was destroyed by an explosion, and 260 of her crew lost their lives. This appalling calamity created intense excitement, but through it all our government kept cool. A Naval Court of Inquiry into the cause of the explosion was at once organized. This Court proceeded to make a thorough investigation on the spot, employing for the purpose a strong force of expert divers and wreckers. After a continuous labor for twenty-three days the Court reached the somewhat indefinite conclusion: "that the loss of the 'Maine' was not in any respect due to fault or negligence on the part of officers or crew * * * the vessel was destroyed by the explosion of a submarine mine situated under the bottom of the ship." The Court was unable to obtain evidence affixing the responsibility "on any person or persons."

The Spanish regarded the presence of the "Maine" at Havana as a menace to Spanish sovereignty on the island, and as an encouragement to the insurgents. The Spanish government asserted that the destruction of the vessel was an accident, due to our own carelessness or negligence, repudiated the findings of our Court of Inquiry, and insisted there was no external explosion, and no Spanish complicity.

By a singular coincidence, as a return of courtesy, the "Viscaya," a very large and heavily-armored cruiser, equipped with the largest guns used in the Spanish navy, arrived in the port of New York. Her captain had no knowledge of the accident (?) to the "Maine." There was an all-around feeling of uneasiness, and her stay was necessarily a short one.

There was a wide-spread belief that the vessel was destroyed by treachery. This was subsequently strengthened, when the maker of the mines (an

Englishman, who sent them to Havana) declared that they could only be exploded through the connivance of the officers who had them in charge. All the evidence showed that the destruction of the "Maine" was no ordinary accident, but was due to external agency and hostile intent, and this formed into

THE OREGON.

quicker fire the glowing coals of righteous wrath, and humanitarian zeal.

Cuban Intervention Resolutions were at once passed by Congress. The Spanish Minister demanded his passports, and left for Canada. An ultimatum embracing these Congressional provisions was forwarded to the Spanish government at Madrid, and next day Spain gave our Minister (Woodward) his passports, thereby severing all diplomatic relations between the two governments.

A fleet was now assembled at Key West. Fifty millions of dollars were voted by Congress as an Emergency Appropriation to be expended according to the President's discretion. Advances of money were made, and scores of private steam yachts of great size and strength were offered to the government by our wealthy citizens. Cuba was now blockaded, many vessels were captured, and several effective bombardments were made on the coast.

The President called for 125,000 volunteers, apportioned through the several States. These responded with cheerfulness and alacrity. On April 25th a state of war was declared to exist, and our Asiatic Squadron under command of Commodore Dewey was ordered from Hong Kong to the Philippines, with instructions to "Capture or destroy the Spanish squadron."

Dewey forced an entrance to Manila Bay on the night of April 30th, and early on the following morning engaged the Spanish fleet which was then under the command of Admiral Montojo. When the battle was over the enemy's fleet had been entirely wiped out, while Dewey's ships had scarcely a scratch. Thirteen vessels were sunk, captured, or burned; three batteries were silenced and destroyed, and a blockade of Manila was established.

This is the most remarkable naval victory on record. Our men went into action with the watchword, "Remember the Maine," and five times they ran along the Spanish line of warships. Not a man on our side was killed, and only eight were injured. Commodore Dewey proved himself a daring and courageous officer. He received the thanks of Congress, and was raised to the rank of Rear-Admiral for this grand victory at Cavite.

ADMIRAL SAMPSON.

A subsequent call was issued for 75,000 additional men. Twenty thousand of these were despatched to take possession of the Philippines, where General Wesley Merritt was appointed Military Governor.

For several weeks our fleet under Admiral Sampson and Commodore Schley scoured the ocean, seeking a Spanish squadron that had been sent from Spain under the command of Admiral Cervera, to succor the Spaniards in Cuba, and to attack our coasts. They, it appears, were short of coal and were hunting at different points for it; hence their manœuvres were veiled in mystery. For a long time they evaded our ships, whose orders were to "Pursue and utterly destroy the Spanish fleet." On May 19th Cer-

COMMODORE SCHLEY.

vera with his six ships stole into Santiago de Cuba. Schley reported the fleet is bottled up in Santiago. "I have got them, and they will never get home." A prediction that was subsequently fulfilled.

Santiago harbor had been mined, and there was danger that any vessel forcing an entrance would meet the fate of the "Maine." Lieutenant Hobson conceived the idea of blocking the channel by sinking a vessel across its mouth, thereby preventing any egress of the Spanish ships. He, with seven men ran the collier "Merrimac" into the harbor and sunk her in the channel, under the fire of the Spanish forts. Hobson and his men were taken prisoners.

LIEUT. HOBSON.

It was a daring exploit, maturely planned and bravely and brilliantly executed. The cool measuring of danger, joined with proud contempt of it; the importance of the end aimed at, and the complete success with which it was attained; the calm ignoring of the terrible risks run, and the entire self-effacement of the young officer and his heroic crew make Lieutenant Hobson's deed one of the most notable in naval annals. The lofty personal bravery of the men woke the admiration of the Spanish Admiral. He did the handsome thing in at once sending out word that our heroes were uninjured, and that he would be glad to restore such brave men to their fleet by exchange.

On June 15th our army sailed for Santiago. General

Shafter took 16,000 men by transports over more than a thousand miles of ocean; landed on a rough coast in the face of an enemy; marched and fought through a tropical jungle thick with hidden foes for days; drove a superior force from entrenched positions on high hills.

Ten days later Cervera was driven out from Santiago. Next day Shafter received the surrender of an army of 18,000 men holding a fortified town. Our loss was less than 250 men.

GENERAL MILES.   GENERAL SHAFTER.

On July 3d, Cervera, acting under orders from General Blanco in Havana, made a gallant dash for liberty. He steamed out with his six fast war ships, and undertook to run away from our fleet. Sampson was away at the time, but Schley who was in command, chased the Spanish ships, fighting them as they ran, until the entire fleet was sunk—four of them being total wrecks. Cervera was taken prisoner, with 1,700 other Spaniards. This gallant action practically wiped out the Spanish navy.

On July 25th our forces landed at Porto Rico. Three days later Ponce, the largest city there, surrendered to General Miles, and he was received with joyful acclamations.

Spain, through the French Ambassador now suggested peace. We went reluctantly into the war and were prepared to make peace any time. The President demanded the independence of Cuba, the cession of Porto Rico, and one of the Ladrones to the United States, and the retention of Manila, pending the final disposition of the Philippines by a joint commission. The demands were acceded to, and the horrible tyranny that was clouding the fairest portions of the earth for three hundred years is brought to an end. With the loss of her naval power and of her colonial empire Spain drops from the ranks of the first-class powers of the world.

Protocols agreeing as to the preliminaries for a treaty of peace were signed on August 12, 1898. Our naval and military commanders were ordered to cease hostilities. The blockades of Cuba, Porto Rico and Manila were lifted, and the war was ended. A new chapter of National history, of world history, is opened before us.

The war opened the door of annexation to Hawaii. President McKinley signed resolutions passed by the Senate annexing the Hawaiian Islands to the United States, and the "Philadelphia" was ordered to Honolulu to raise the American flag, which had been hauled down under Cleveland's direction in 1893.

NO.	PRESIDENT.	STATE.	TERM OF OFFICE.	BY WHOM ELECTED.
1	George Washington	Virginia	Two terms; 1789-1797	Whole people
2	John Adams	Massachusetts	One term; 1797-1801	Federalists
3	Thomas Jefferson	Virginia	Two terms; 1801-1809	Republicans
4	James Madison	Virginia	Two terms; 1809-1817	Republicans
5	James Monroe	Virginia	Two terms; 1817-1825	All parties
6	John Quincy Adams	Massachusetts	One term; 1825-1829	House of Rep
7	Andrew Jackson	Tennessee	Two terms; 1829-1837	Democrats
8	Martin Van Buren	New York	One term; 1837-1841	Democrats
9	William H. Harrison	Ohio	One month; 1841	Whigs
10	John Tyler	Virginia	3 years and 11 months	Whigs
11	James K. Polk	Tennessee	One term; 1845-1849	Democrats
12	Zachary Taylor	Louisiana	1 year and 4 months	Whigs
13	Millard Fillmore	New York	2 years and 8 months	Whigs
14	Franklin Pierce	New Hampshire	One term; 1853-1857	Democrats
15	James Buchanan	Pennsylvania	One term; 1857-1861	Democrats
16	Abraham Lincoln	Illinois	One term and 1 month	Republicans
17	Andrew Johnson	Tennessee	3 years and 11 months	Republicans
18	Ulysses S. Grant	Illinois	Two terms; 1869-1877	Republicans
19	Rutherford B. Hayes	Ohio	One term; 1877-1881	Republicans
20	James A. Garfield	Ohio	6 months and 15 days	Republicans
21	Chester A. Arthur	New York	3 years and 5 months	Republicans
22	Grover Cleveland	New York	One term; 1885-1889	Democrats
23	Benjamin Harrison	Indiana	One term; 1889-1893	Republicans
24	Grover Cleveland	New York	One term (2d); 1893-1897	Democrats
25	William McKinley	Ohio		Republicans

TABLE OF ADMISSION OF STATES.

1	Delaware	accepted the Constitution		Dec. 7,	1787
2	Pennsylvania	" " "		Dec. 12,	1787
3	New Jersey	" " "		Dec. 18,	1787
4	Georgia	" " "		Jan. 2,	1788
5	Connecticut	" " "		Jan. 9,	1788
6	Massachusetts	" " "		Feb. 6,	1788
7	Maryland	" " "		Apr. 28,	1788
8	South Carolina	" " "		May 23,	1788
9	New Hampshire	" " "		June 21,	1788
10	Virginia	" " "		June 25,	1788
11	New York	" " "		July 26,	1788
12	North Carolina	" " "		Nov. 21,	1789
13	Rhode Island	" " "		May 29,	1790
14	Vermont	admitted to the Union		Mar. 4,	1791
15	Kentucky	" " "		June 1,	1792
16	Tennessee	" " "		June 1,	1796
17	Ohio	" " "		Nov. 29,	1802
18	Louisiana	" " "		Apr. 30,	1812
19	Indiana	" " "		Dec. 11,	1816
20	Mississippi	" " "		Dec. 10,	1817
21	Illinois	" " "		Dec. 3,	1818
22	Alabama	" " "		Dec. 14,	1819
23	Maine	" " "		Mar. 15,	1820
24	Missouri	" " "		Aug. 10,	1821
25	Arkansas	" " "		June 15,	1836
26	Michigan	" " "		Jan. 26,	1837
27	Florida	" " "		Mar. 3,	1845
28	Texas	" " "		Dec. 29,	1845
29	Iowa	" " "		Dec. 28,	1846
30	Wisconsin	" " "		May 29,	1848
31	California	" " "		Sept. 9,	1850
32	Minnesota	" " "		May 11,	1858
33	Oregon	" " "		Feb. 14,	1859
34	Kansas	" " "		Jan. 29,	1861
35	West Virginia	" " "		June 19,	1863
36	Nevada	" " "		Oct. 31,	1864
37	Nebraska	" " "		Mar. 1,	1867
38	Colorado	" " "		Aug. 1,	1876
39	North Dakota	" " "		Feb. 22,	1889
40	South Dakota	" " "		Feb. 22,	1889
41	Montana	" " "		Feb. 22,	1889
42	Washington	" " "		Feb. 22,	1889
43	Idaho	" " "		July 3,	1890
44	Wyoming	" " "		July 11,	1890
45	Utah	" " "		Jan. 4,	1896

ALTEMUS' YOUNG PEOPLE'S LIBRARY.

ROBINSON CRUSOE: His Life and Strange, Surprising Adventures. With 70 beautiful illustrations by WALTER PAGET.

"Was there ever anything written that the reader wished longer except ROBINSON CRUSOE and PILGRIM'S PROGRESS?"—*Samuel Johnson.*

"There exists no work, either of instruction or entertainment, which has been more generally read, and universally admired."—*Walter Scott.*

ALICE'S ADVENTURES IN WONDERLAND. With 42 illustrations by JOHN TENNIEL.

"Lewis Carroll's immortal story."—*Athenæum.*

"The most delightful of children's stories. Elegant and delicious nonsense."—*Saturday Review.*

THROUGH THE LOOKING GLASS AND WHAT ALICE FOUND THERE. (*A companion to* ALICE IN WONDERLAND.) With 50 illustrations by JOHN TENNIEL.

"Will fairly rank with the tale of her previous experience."—*Daily Telegraph.* . . . "Many of Tenniel's designs are masterpieces of wise absurdity."—*Athenæum.* . . . "Not a whit inferior to its predecessor in grand extravagance of imagination, and delicious allegorical nonsense."—*Quarterly Review.*

BUNYAN'S PILGRIM'S PROGRESS. With 50 full-page and text illustrations.

PILGRIM'S PROGRESS is the most popular story book in the world. With the exception of the Bible it has been translated into more languages than any other book ever printed.

A CHILD'S STORY OF THE BIBLE. With 72 full-page illustrations.

Tells in simple language and in a form fitted for the hands of the younger members of the Christian flock, the tale of God's dealings with his Chosen People under the Old Dispensation, with its foreshadowings of the coming of that Messiah who was to make all mankind one fold under one Shepherd.

A CHILD'S LIFE OF CHRIST. With 49 illustrations.

God has implanted in the infant heart a desire to hear of Jesus, and children are early attracted and sweetly riveted by the wonderful Story of the Master from the Manger to the Throne.

In this little book we have brought together from Scripture every incident, expression and description, within the verge of their comprehension in the effort to weave them into a memorial garland of their Saviour.

CHRISTOPHER COLUMBUS AND THE DISCOVERY OF AMERICA. With 70 illustrations.

It is the duty of every American lad to know the story of Christopher Columbus. In this book is depicted the story of his life and struggles; of his persistent solicitations at the Courts of Europe, and his contemptuous receptions by the learned Geographical Councils, until his final employment by Queen Isabella. Records the day-by-day journeyings while he was pursuing his aim and perilous way over the shoreless Ocean, until he "gave to Spain a New World." Shows his progress through Spain on the occasion of his first return, when he was received with rapturous demonstrations and more than regal homage. His displacement by the Odjeas, Ovandos and Bobadilas; his last return in chains, and the story of his death in poverty and neglect.

One distinguishing feature of this edition is, that many of the illustrations are copies from DeBry's and Herrara's histories, which were compiled by authority of the King of Spain, showing the Indians, in their life and customs, as they appeared to the early discoverers.

LIVES OF THE PRESIDENTS OF THE UNITED STATES. Compiled from authoritative sources. With portraits of the Presidents; and also of the unsuccessful candidates for the office; as well as the ablest of the Cabinet officers.

This book should be in every home and school library. It tells, in an impartial way, the story of the political history of the United States, from the first Constitutional convention till the last Presidential nominations. It is *just the book* for intelligent boys, and it will help to make them intelligent and patriotic citizens.

GULLIVER'S TRAVELS INTO SOME REMOTE REGIONS OF THE WORLD. With 50 illustrations.

In description, even of the most common-place things, his power is often perfectly marvellous. Macaulay says of SWIFT: "Under a plain garb and ungainly deportment were concealed some of the choicest gifts that ever have been bestowed on any of the children of men,—rare powers of observation, brilliant art, grotesque invention, humor of the most austere flavor, yet exquisitely delicious, eloquence singularly pure, manly, and perspicuous."

MOTHER GOOSE'S RHYMES, JINGLES, AND FAIRY TALES. With 300 illustrations.

"In this edition an excellent choice has been made from the standard fiction of the little ones. The abundant pictures are well drawn and graceful, the effect frequently striking and always decorative."—*Critic.*
. . . "Only to see the book is to wish to give it to every child one knows."—*Queen.*

THE FABLES OF ÆSOP. Compiled from the best accepted sources. With 62 illustrations.

The fables of Æsop are among the very earliest compositions of this kind, and probably have never been surpassed for point and brevity, as well as for the practical good sense they display. In their grotesque grace, in their quaint humor, in their trust in the simpler virtues, in their insight into the cruder vices, in their innocence of the fact of sex, ÆSOP'S FABLES are as little children—and for that reason they will ever find a home in the heaven of little children's souls.

THE STORY OF ADVENTURE IN THE FROZEN SEAS. With 70 illustrations. Compiled from authorized sources.

We have here brought together the records of the attempts to reach the North Pole. Our object being to recall the stories of the early voyagers, and to narrate the recent efforts of gallant adventurers of various nationalities to cross the "unknown and inaccessible" threshold; and to show how much can be accomplished by indomitable pluck and steady perseverance. Portraits and numerous illustrations help the narration.

The North Polar region is the largest, as it is the most important field of discovery that remains for this generation to work out. As Frobisher declared nearly three hundred and fifty years ago, it is "the only great thing left undone in the world." Every year diminishes the extent of the unknown; and there is a bare likelihood that Dr. Nansen has already explored the hitherto unexplorable.

THE STORY OF EXPLORATION AND DISCOVERY IN AFRICA. With 80 illustrations.

Records the experiences of adventures, privations, sufferings, trials, dangers, and discoveries in developing the "Dark Continent," from the early days of Bruce and Mungo Park down to Livingstone and Stanley and the heroes of our own times.

The reader becomes carried away by conflicting emotions of wonder and sympathy, and feels compelled to pursue the story, which he cannot lay down. No present can be more acceptable than such a volume as this, where courage, intrepidity, resource and devotion are so pleasantly mingled. It is very fully illustrated with pictures worthy of the book.

THE SWISS FAMILY ROBINSON, or the Adventures of a Shipwrecked Family on an Uninhabited Island. With 50 illustrations.

A remarkable tale of adventure that will interest the boys and girls. The father of the family tells the tale and the vicissitudes through which he and his wife and children pass, the wonderful discoveries they make, and the dangers they encounter. It is a standard work of adventure that has the favor of all who have read it.

THE ARABIAN NIGHTS ENTERTAINMENTS. With 50 illustrations. Contains the most favorably known of the stories.

The text is somewhat abridged and edited for the young. It forms an excellent introduction to those immortal tales which have helped so long to keep the weary world young.

ILLUSTRATED NATURAL HISTORY. By the Rev. J. G. Wood. With 80 illustrations.

Wood's Natural History needs no commendation. Its author has done more than any other writer to popularize the study. His work is known and admired over all the civilized world. The sales of his works in England and America have been enormous. The illustrations in this edition are entirely new, striking, and life-like.

A CHILD'S HISTORY OF ENGLAND. By Charles Dickens. With 50 illustrations.

Dickens grew tired of listening to his children memorizing the old-fashioned twaddle that went under the name of English history. He thereupon wrote a book, in his own peculiarly happy style, primarily for the educational advantage of his own children, but was prevailed upon to publish the work, and make its use general. Its success was instantaneous and abiding.

BLACK BEAUTY; The Autobiography of a Horse. By Anna Sewell. With 50 illustrations.

This NEW ILLUSTRATED EDITION is sure to command attention. Wherever children are, whether boys or girls, there this Autobiography should be. It inculcates habits of kindness to all members of the animal creation. The literary merit of the book is excellent.

GRIMM'S FAIRY TALES. With 50 Illustrations.

These Tales of the Brothers Grimm have carried their names into every household of the civilized world.
The Tales are a wonderful collection, as interesting, from a literary point of view, as they are delightful as stories.

ANDERSEN'S FAIRY TALES. By Hans Christian Andersen. With 77 illustrations.

The spirit of high moral teaching, and the delicacy of sentiment, feeling, and expression that pervade these tales make these wonderful creations not only attractive to the young, but equally acceptable to those of mature years, who are able to understand their real significance and appreciate the depth of their meaning.

FLOWER FABLES. By Louisa May Alcott. With colored and plain illustrations.

A series of very interesting fairy tales by the most charming of American story-tellers.

GRANDFATHER'S CHAIR: A History for Youth. By Nathaniel Hawthorne. With 60 illustrations.

The story of America from the landing of the Puritans to the *acknowledgment without reserve* of the Independence of the United States, told with all the elegance, simplicity, grace, clearness, and force for which Hawthorne is conspicuously noted.

www.ingramcontent.com/pod-product-compliance
Lightning Source LLC
Chambersburg PA
CBHW032110230426
43672CB00009B/1692